THE LEGEND OF
GULFSTREAM

THE LEGEND OF GULFSTREAM

JEFFREY L. RODENGEN

Edited by Alex Lieber
Design and layout by Sandy Cruz

For Roger Tyzzer, J.J.J.,
a friendship in perpetual climb.

WRITE STUFF

Write Stuff Enterprises, Inc.
1001 South Andrews Avenue, Second Floor
Fort Lauderdale, FL 33316
1-800-900-Book (1-800-900-2665)
(954) 462-6657
www.writestuffbooks.com

Publisher's Cataloging in Publication

Rodengen, Jeffrey L.
    The legend of Gulfstream/Jeffrey L.
Rodengen. – 1st ed.
        p. cm.
        Includes bibliographical references and index.
        ISBN 0-945903-62-6
Rodengen. – 1st ed.
        1. Gulfstream Aerospace Corporation –
History 2. Aircraft industry – United States –
History. 3. industry – United States – History.
I. Title.

HD9711.U63G85 2000
338.7/6291334/0973   QBI99-1556

Library of Congress
Catalog Card Number 99-76491

ISBN 0-945903-62-6

Completely produced in the
United States of America
10 9 8 7 6 5 4 3 2 1

Also by Jeff Rodengen

The Legend of Chris-Craft

*IRON FIST: The Lives
of Carl Kiekhaefer*

*Evinrude-Johnson and
The Legend of OMC*

*Serving the Silent Service:
The Legend of Electric Boat*

*The Legend of
Dr Pepper/Seven-Up*

The Legend of Honeywell

*The Legend of
Briggs & Stratton*

The Legend of Ingersoll-Rand

*The Legend of Stanley:
150 Years of The Stanley Works*

The MicroAge Way

The Legend of Halliburton

*The Legend of
York International*

*The Legend of
Nucor Corporation*

*The Legend of Goodyear:
The First 100 Years*

The Legend of AMP

The Legend of Cessna

The Legend of VF Corporation

The Spirit of AMD

*New Horizons:
The Story of Ashland Inc.*

The Legend of Rowan

*The History of
American Standard*

The Legend of Mercury Marine

The Legend of Federal-Mogul

*Against the Odds:
Inter-Tel—The First 30 Years*

The Legend of Pfizer

*State of the Heart:
The Practical Guide to
Your Heart and Heart Surgery*
with Larry W. Stephenson, M.D.

*The Legend of
Worthington Industries*

*The Legend of
Trinity Industries, Inc.*

The Legend of IBP, Inc.

*The Legend of
Cornelius Vanderbilt Whitney*

The Legend of Amdahl

The Legend of Litton Industries

The Legend of Bertram

TABLE OF CONTENTS

FOREWORD

BY

HENRY KISSINGER
FORMER SECRETARY OF STATE

Henry Kissinger was the U.S. Secretary of State from 1973 to 1977, and a national security adviser to presidents Richard Nixon and Gerald Ford. He accompanied Nixon on his historic 1972 visit to China, and he shared the Nobel Peace Prize in 1973 for negotiating a cease-fire with North Vietnam. He has written several books on foreign policy and two volumes of memoirs.

IT'S DIFFICULT FOR ME TO calculate how many flights or how many miles I have flown aboard Gulfstream aircraft. I have been completely around the world on them on a number of occasions. Being aboard these large, effecient, fast and elegant aircraft has made many of the millions of miles I have flown a pleasure, as well as very productive. I am more accustomed, as those of you who have followed my career in public service may surmise, to comment on the evolution of foreign policy than on a global leader in business. As a former member of the board of directors, and as one who had witnessed the results that passionate leadership and dedicated teamwork can achieve, I believe I can contribute a unique perspective.

Following a chance meeting at the funeral of Princess Diana, I accepted Teddy Forstmann's invitation to join the board of Gulfstream Aerospace Corporation. It was one of the most unusual boards, as it included well-known names in industry, public service and the military, and among them were dear friends of many years. My fellow board members included former Chairman of the Joint Chiefs of Staff General Colin Powell, fellow former Secretary of State George Schultz, Roger S. Penske, chairman, Penske Corporation, Michael Ovitz, former chairman, Create Artists Agency, and many others.

It was a unique opportunity for each of us to meet periodically, not only to monitor the remarkable progress of Gulfstream, but to also compare notes on events of national and international importance. Each to our abilities, we also helped to spread the word of Gulfstream's revival throughout the world or our contacts and colleagues. When we met for the last time at a restaurant in New York, it was a melancholy farewell as a group, as we had all enjoyed our tenures on the board, and many proposals were advanced for a reunion one day.

Prominent among my memories of my term on the board was the personal sacrifice and professional risk that Teddy Forstmann of the investment group Forstmann Little assumed during a crucial period of uncertainty and transition. Assuming the role of CEO at a time when even some of his own investors cautioned otherwise, Teddy challenged both the organization and the marketplace to accept nothing less than the highest quality and the greatest performance. He believed deeply in the staying power of the Gulfstream brand name and its ability to survive hardship. Teddy's ability to redirect resources, recruit exciting new leadership and inspire the organization to higher goals was rewarding for those of us on the board to observe.

Even though my duties on the board of Gulfstream have expired, I will continue to be reminded of the great works of the company as I travel throughout the world.

UNITED STATES OF AMERICA

ACKNOWLEDGMENTS

A GREAT NUMBER OF PEO-ple assisted in the research, preparation, and publication of *The Legend of Gulfstream*. The principal research and narrative timeline were accomplished by my talented and enterprising research assistant Lynda Natali.

The project wouldn't have gotten off the ground without Long Island's Grumman History Center and the kind and generous support of retired Grumman historians Lawrence Feliu, Michael Hlinko, and Roger Seybel. Thanks also to Sandy James, the daughter of a Grummanite and a valued member of Gulfstream's team, and to Kelly Holland, another Gulfstream public relations pro. Keith Mordoff, director of corporate communications, and Missy Henderson, senior administrative associate, were instrumental in helping the project run smoothly. The Gulfstream Retiree Club was invaluable, and special thanks to Cindy Collins for introducing Ms. Natali to it. Thanks to Mr. and Mrs. Dan Murphy and Mr. and Mrs. Bill Bauer for sharing stories, and to Rob Wolz for boxes filled with great stuff. I would also like to thank Gulfstream engineering librarians Ann Duzansky and Mary Pitt; department head Sandra Hayden-Henry; and Al Tebbetts and Debra Youles in Gulfstream's photo department. For their generosity in lending photos for the book, my thanks go to *Air Force Magazine*, Joseph Anckner, Bob Coman, Bob Cooper, Charles Coppi, Albert "Goldie" Glenn, Earl Schaeffer, Herman Schonenberg, Robert Smyth, and George Viteritti.

This work would not have been possible without the candid insights of many Gulfstream executives, employees, board members, and retirees. I am indebted to Joseph Anckner, retired group leader in charge of the GII mock-up and also an international salesman; Bob Anderson, chairman emeritus of Rockwell Corporation and a Gulfstream board director; Ira Berman, general counsel; Thomas Bell, president and CEO of Burson-Marsteller and a Gulfstream board director; Bill Boisture, president and COO; Fred Breidenbach, retired president and COO; Ken Burckhardt, senior vice president of finance; Bob Coman, retired director of Gulfstream's C-20 program; Charles Coppi, retired senior vice president of engineering; Knoxie Crocker, coordinator and inspector of electrical installation; Chris Davis, former executive vice president and CFO; Ed Flinn, director of flight sciences; Larry Flynn, senior vice president in charge of Aircraft Services; Ted Forstmann, chairman and CEO; Bill Gentzingler, retired project manager for the nacelle and thrust reversers for the F-100 and GIV; Albert "Goldie" Glenn, retired vice chairman; Marsha Grovenstein, vice president of customer service; Pres Henne, senior vice president of programs; Sandra Horbach, Forstmann Little & Company general partner; Steven Hunt, project director for small engines at Rolls-Royce; Ken Lilley, head of marketing small engines at Rolls-Royce; Ted Mendenhall, test pilot; Russ Meyer, former president and CEO of American Aviation; Bryan Moss, vice chairman; Michael Ovitz, former chairman and co-owner of Creative Artists Agency and a Gulfstream board director; Allen Paulson, retired chairman and CEO; Roger Penske, chairman and CEO of Penske Corporation and a Gulfstream board director; Colin Powell, former chairman of the joint chiefs of staff and a Gulfstream board director; Sir Ralph Robins, managing director for Rolls-Royce; Gerard Roche, chairman of Heidrick & Struggles and a Gulfstream board director; Don Rumsfeld, former secretary of defense and a Gulfstream board director; Earl Schaeffer, retired flight trainer; Herman Schonenberg, retired director of materials at the Bethpage plant; Robert Smyth, retired vice president of flight operations and quality control; Robert Strauss, former U.S. ambassador to Russia, founder and partner of Akin, Gump, Strauss, Hauer & Feld, and a Gulfstream board director; Peter Viemeister, retired vice president of development for Grumman Aerospace; George Viteritti, retired director of engineering; and Joe Walker, senior vice president of worldwide sales.

As always, the author extends a special thanks to the dedicated team at Write Stuff Enterprises, Inc.: Alex Lieber, former executive editor; Jon VanZile, executive editor; Melody Maysonet, senior editor; Heather Cohn and Marie Etzler, associate editors; Sandy Cruz, senior art director; Jill Apolinario, Rachelle Donley, Wendy Iverson, Joey Henderson, and Dennis Shockley, art directors; Amanda Fowler, assistant to the author; Fred Moll, production manager; David Patten and Tony Wall, executive authors; Bonnie Freeman, proofreader; Mary Aaron, transcriptionist; Erica Orloff, indexer; Marianne Roberts, office manager; Bonnie Bratton, director of marketing; Grace Kurotori, sales and promotions manager; Rafael Santiago, logistics specialist; and Karine Rodengen, project coordinator.

1937
Grumman Aircraft introduces the Goose, the first commercial aircraft ever built by the company.

1946
Grumman introduces the Mallard, a legendary amphibious aircraft that meets with only modest success.

1957
Design of the Gulfstream I begins.

1958
The first flight of the turboprop-driven GI takes place on August 14.

1959
The GI gains FAA approval on May 21.

1965
The go-ahead is given in May for the GII, a jet-powered successor to the GI.

1966
The GII takes its first flight on October 2.

1967
Grumman moves the Gulfstream program to Savannah, Georgia.

1967
The GII gains FAA approval on October 19.

1968
The GII becomes the first corporate/business aircraft to cross the Atlantic nonstop, covering 3,500 miles from Teterboro, New Jersey, to London, England.

1972
Grumman merges the Gulfstream program with American Aviation of Cleveland, Ohio, to form Grumman American Aviation. Russ Meyer becomes president of the new Grumman subsidiary.

1973
NASA orders two GIIs to be used as Space Shuttle trainers.

1976
Design concept for the GIII is unveiled, but development is stopped a year later.

1977
Work begins on a scaled-down version of the GIII.

Grumman G-44A—
the 1948 WIDGEON

The Widgeon, offspring of the Grumman Goose, represented Grumman's first attempt to build an aircraft solely for commercial use. *(Photo courtesy of Albert Glenn.)*

CHAPTER ONE

IN PEACE AND WAR

1910–1957

*"I wouldn't mind building another commercial airplane before I retire.
Heck, I'd like to do one rather than keep doing these weapon systems."*

— Leroy Grumman, 1955[1]

ON AUGUST 14, 1958, A new era in the history of aviation was born when test pilots Carl Alber and Fred Rowley lifted the first Gulfstream into the sky. The story that followed was one of technological breakthroughs and world-class performance by the men and women who eventually comprised Gulfstream Aerospace.

The history of Gulfstream actually begins when aviation was in its infancy and the connection between business and aviation was just starting to form. The year was 1910, and seven years had passed since Wilbur and Orville Wright made the world's first successful powered flight at Kitty Hawk, North Carolina. The brothers had continued their passion for aviation after making their historic flight and, fittingly, it was they who made what is believed to be the first business trip ever taken via aircraft. A man named Max Morehouse, the owner of a dry-goods store in Ohio, hired the Wright brothers to transport two packages of silk from Dayton to Columbus. The flight and the flying exhibition which took place after the silk was delivered were heavily publicized. Thousands showed up and gladly paid $1 to see the Wright Model B biplane make the delivery, inspiring scores of others to build and fly homemade craft.[2]

In these early years the aircraft had no truly commercial role other than that of stunt flying and events designed to generate publicity. In 1919, the Heddon Company of Dowagiac, Michigan, painted the fuselage of its JN-4D Curtiss Jenny biplane — a surplus World War I training aircraft — to look like a fish to help sell its line of fishing lures.[3] The public's interest in flying was further enhanced by the popularity of barnstormers. These "flying gypsies," as they were known, traveled from town to village earning a living any way possible, from passenger rides to stunt flying. In the twenties, organized crime was among the first enterprises to appreciate the advantage of using aircraft as business tools; smugglers often transported bootleg liquor by plane during Prohibition.[4]

The usefulness of aircraft was also perceived by a few visionaries in government. Postmaster General Otto Praeger, conscious of the Post Office's vow of speedy and reliable service, had been a passionate advocate of airmail since 1916 but was thwarted by opposition in Congress and World War I. His vision was fulfilled in May 1918, when two post office clerks successfully delivered

The Grumman Aircraft Engineering Company was launched on January 2, 1930, in a rented garage. In the beginning, the founders shrewdly focused on military contracts. *(Photo courtesy of the Grumman History Center.)*

Above: The 1925 Kelly Act opened new roles for airplanes. This Cessna Type 500, operated by National Air Transport, was modified to transport mail on the Chicago-Dallas route. *(Photo courtesy of Cessna.)*

Below: Halliburton's S.A.F.E.Way airline flew to points east and west without radar, radios or current weather reports but still maintained an impressive safety record. The Great Depression doomed the fledgling airline, however. *(Photo courtesy of Halliburton Company.)*

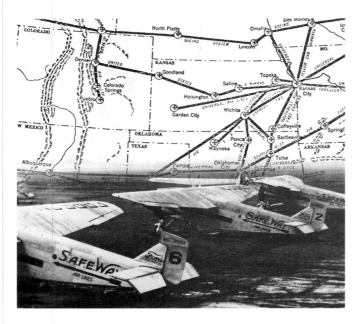

airmail from New York to Washington, D.C. Undeniably successful, airmail was officially established in August 1918. In 1925, Congress passed the Kelly Act, which encouraged private companies to haul mail.[5]

In the field of private — and legal — enterprise, the regular use of aircraft was slow to develop as a business tool, but Charles Lindbergh's epic crossing of the Atlantic Ocean in 1927 gave the aircraft industry a boost by demonstrating that flight was becoming safe and reliable. Oil business executives were among the first to recognize its promise. Following Lindbergh's flight, the Standard Oil Company of Indiana purchased a Ford Tri-Motor, a high-wing, three-engine aircraft produced by Ford Motor Company. Capable of carrying up to 12 passengers, the sturdy Tri-Motor permitted Standard Oil business executives to perform on-site inspections of the company's oil fields.[6] Other oil and oil-related companies followed suit. The founder and owner of Halliburton Oil Well Cementing Company, Erle Halliburton, even went so far as to establish a regular passenger route called S.A.F.E.Way using the proven Ford Tri-Motor.

However, the Tri-Motor was devoid of creature comforts. Cold and uncomfortable, the aircraft was also hard to handle because it was designed to fit Henry Ford's famous mass-production process rather than the laws of aerodynamics. The onset of the Great Depression, which consumed the hope and livelihoods of millions of people, was the death knell of the Ford Tri-Motor, Halliburton's S.A.F.E.Way passenger line and many of the pioneer commercial aircraft manufacturers, such as the Cessna Aircraft Company.[7]

The Lockheed Vega was another aircraft that achieved early distinction as a commercial aircraft. Built in 1927, the single-engine Vega was designed by John Northrop, a self-taught designer who went on to found Northrop Corporation. Made almost entirely of wood, the Vega seated up to seven people and was designed as a light transport. The interior could be modified to become a flying office, complete with typewriters and even a lavatory.

The Vega set and broke a number of records. Flown by famous fliers such as Wiley Post and Amelia Earhart, the streamlined Vega was capable

of speeds of 180 miles an hour and could travel more than 690 miles. Fledgling airline companies used the airplane because of its range and seating capacity. As with the Tri-Motor, production of the Vega stopped as a result of the Great Depression.

The setback was temporary because the airplane had proven itself a valuable business tool, according to Roger Bilstein, author of the authoritative *The American Aerospace Industry*.

"Through the 1920s and early 1930s, the Fords and similar types from Boeing served as the advance guard.... Movie stars and public figures became regular patrons, adding glamour and a cosmopolitan flavor to air travel. More importantly, larger numbers of business people took to the airways as a means of saving time and maximizing their effectiveness."[8]

But general aviation's true turning point came with the beginning of World War II in 1939 and the entry of the United States in December 1941. The war's impact on general aviation in the United States cannot be overstated, even though civilian production was suspended for the duration. In

The Lockheed Vega, designed as a seven-place light transport, broke numerous long-distance and speed records. The *Winnie Mae*, piloted by the famed aviator Wiley Post, completed the first around-the-world solo flight. *(Illustration by Sandy Cruz.)*

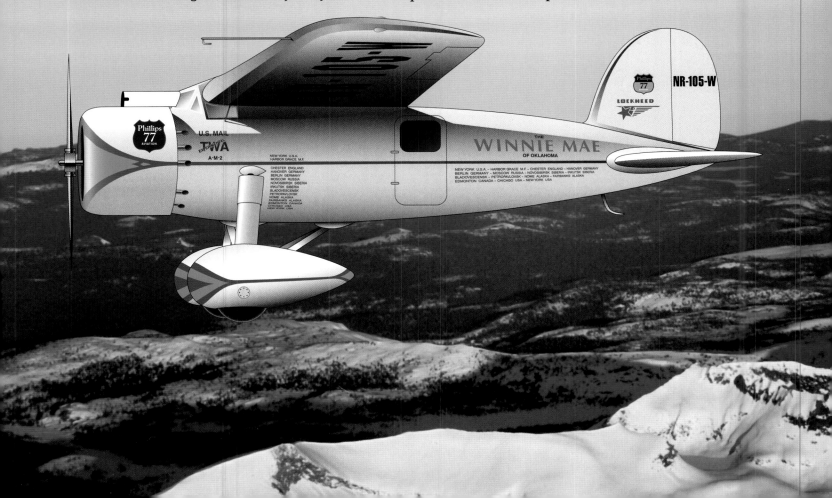

1939, American factories built fewer than 6,000 aircraft. By 1944, aircraft production neared 100,000 units of every description, with technology improving dramatically under the exigencies of wartime production. Turbine engines, vastly improved radar, transponders and the autopilot were just a few of the major advances that emerged from the conflict.

In addition, thousands of young military pilots and aircraft mechanics were destined to return at war's end to a nation about to experience the greatest period of prosperity in world history.[9] The postwar optimism that flourished contributed to the rise in civil aircraft production. Forecasts for the private aviation market, especially light air-

craft, were strong, and aircraft ads appeared in publications as diverse as *Business Week* and *Better Homes and Gardens*.[10] The federal government predicted that production would increase to more than 200,000 aircraft a year.

Although the idea of an airplane for every household never materialized, another change was taking place after World War II that would have a lasting impact on the development of aviation. The rise of the conglomerate in the 1950s required extensive travel, often on short notice, by executives with a need to visit their far-flung holdings and operations. That need would be met by the Grumman Aircraft Engineering Company in a risky yet innovative push into the civilian aircraft market. But first Grumman had to surmount two of the most cataclysmic events in world history, the Great Depression and World War II.

The Grumman Aircraft Engineering Company

The Grumman Aircraft Engineering Company began in a small rented garage on the south shore of Long Island in Baldwin, New York. Leroy Grumman and a small group of friends that included Bill Schwendler and Leon "Jake" Swirbul, all from the defunct Loening Aeronautical Engineering Corporation, mortgaged their houses, borrowed from relatives and threw in their savings to raise the money needed to get their aircraft repair business running.[11] On January 2, 1930, they opened for business. Their first piece of work was literally dragged into the garage by Leroy Grumman: a damaged Loening amphibian aircraft, which they repaired and sold.

On the surface, it appeared that the men couldn't have picked a worse time to start a business, but they shielded themselves from the economic maelstrom by focusing strictly on military contracts. In fact, they couldn't have picked a better time because the federal government was

Leroy Grumman, left, and Jake Swirbul were two of the seven founders of the Grumman Aircraft Engineering Company. They are shown here standing next to the company's first Widgeon in the summer of 1940. *(Photo courtesy of the Grumman History Center.)*

The XFF-1 was the first airplane built by Grumman. Nicknamed "FiFi," this tough airplane was the Navy's first fighter to use retractable landing gear. *(Photo courtesy of the Grumman History Center.)*

seeking ways to bolster the economy, and the military was experimenting with aircraft that could be launched from both the decks of aircraft carriers and the landing fields of fixed island bases.

The company's first contract was to design and build a single amphibious float with retractable landing gear for testing on the Navy's Vought Corsair biplanes, amphibious aircraft used for scouting and observation missions.[12] Retractable landing gear was a relatively new feature at that time, having been introduced in 1922. Consequently, the first designs were heavy and prone to malfunction. The men had been working on a lighter, more reliable gear to retract the wheels and park them within the fuselage of the aircraft.[13] Grumman developed the landing gear, but the company was determined to advance beyond just supplying components to cumbersome aircraft like an amphibian. It was determined to design and build first-line military aircraft.

On April 2, 1931, a little over a year after opening for business, Grumman won its first contract to build a new airplane. Designated the XFF-1 (and nicknamed "FiFi"), it was the first Navy fighter to use retractable landing gear.[14] The two-seated FiFi fighter was not as cute or gentle as the

name implied. In fact, it was quite the opposite. Rugged and dependable, the stubby biplane possessed the features that would later make the Grumman F4F Wildcat famous. It handled well at low speeds and yet was tough enough to endure the pounding that comes with landing on the heaving deck of an aircraft carrier. Its small size, furthermore, was ideal for the limited space on the deck or in the hangar of carriers.

The FiFi fighter was accepted by the Navy, and its orders enabled Grumman Aircraft to expand out of the garage in Baldwin and into a factory at Valley Stream, Long Island, on the edge of Curtiss Field. By now, employment had risen to 42, and the workforce was busy meeting orders for the FiFi fighter and Model B float planes. A year later, Grumman relocated to Farmingdale, which was about 12 miles east of Valley Stream on Long Island.

By the end of 1934, the workforce had mushroomed to more than 220 and the company achieved $1 million in sales for the first time. With the development of successor aircraft like the F2F and F3F, Grumman had a lock on the naval aircraft market. In 1936, Grumman Aircraft moved several miles northwest to its permanent home at Bethpage, Long Island.

That year was momentous for another reason: It saw the introduction of the F4F prototype. Though several years of at times frustrating design work lay ahead, the Grumman Wildcat was destined to secure a place in military aviation history.

In Time of Peace

The year of the Wildcat was also the year Roy Grumman decided to diversify into the commercial aviation market. Grumman was still primarily involved with developing military aircraft but made several important strides into commercial aviation during this period.

In 1936, a group of 10 wealthy sportsmen/businessmen (including Henry Morgan, Cornelius Vanderbilt Whitney, Marshall Field and E.R. Harriman) expressed an interest in the development of an amphibian aircraft with the capacity to reach a variety of locations from remote fishing lakes to small dirt fields and snow-covered roads.[15] During this time in the development of general aviation, water was more likely than airstrips to be available for landing, so amphibians were popular aircraft.[16]

The Grumman Model G-21 Goose was the result. This eight-person, twin-engine amphibian had a top speed of 215 miles per hour and range of about 750 statute miles.[17] Among its distinguishing characteristics was the hand-cranked retractable undercarriage that could be used for land operations or in the water during beachings.

The Goose was the brainchild of a number of wealthy men who wanted to develop a versatile amphibian airplane for business and recreational purposes. The Grumman Goose was better received by the military than by the civilian market, however. *(Photo courtesy of Charles Coppi.)*

For operations from snow-covered fields, the main and tail wheels could be replaced with skis.[18]

The Grumman Goose was first flown in May 1937. However, despite its outstanding performance, the company initially built just 10 of the aircraft for commercial use. Eventually, the military acknowledged the versatility of the Goose and purchased 345 aircraft for use by the Army, Navy and Coast Guard.[19]

Three years after the debut of the Goose, Grumman realized there was a commercial need for a smaller version of the Goose. Thus was born the Grumman G-44 Widgeon, an aircraft that was strikingly similar to the Goose except that the baby version was designed with an angular tail surface and in-line engines. The average Widgeon had two seats in the cockpit and up to four in the cabin. As was the case with the Goose,

CHAPTER ONE: IN PEACE AND WAR

it wasn't long before the military became the Widgeon's biggest customer, along with a handful of foreign nations, Great Britain among them. The British military, paying deference to its older and larger sibling, called its Widgeons "Goslings."[20] This type of aircraft served in many roles during World War II, including those of courier, patrol, light transport, airsea rescue and antisubmarine warfare. In fact, the U.S. Coast Guard scored its first kill of an enemy submarine with a Widgeon when a member of Squadron 212 sank a German U-boat in the Gulf of Mexico.[21]

In 1938, the company went public. That year, the F4F fighter, known as the Wildcat, went into full production for the Navy.

In Time of War

On December 7, 1941, more than 360 Japanese aircraft launched from an aircraft carrier task force attacked the unsuspecting U.S. Pacific fleet at Pearl Harbor. The attack killed more than 2,400 Americans, sank or heavily damaged eight battleships — the pride of the American fleet — and destroyed more than 170 aircraft on the ground.

With the battleships out of action, the United States had no choice but to embrace a strategy that emphasized the aircraft carrier battle group. Fortunately, the American carriers had left Pearl Harbor before the attack.

The concept of the carrier battle group had been in development since the earliest days of aviation, when a Curtiss-Wright aircraft flew off the scout cruiser USS *Birmingham* in 1910. In World War I, aircraft carriers were used mainly to launch scout planes. By World War II, however, tactics had been developed that turned a carrier's complement of aircraft into a decisive weapon, as demonstrated by the attack on Pearl Harbor.

Naval combat changed in concept forever during the Battle of the Coral Sea in 1942. The Japanese were attempting to capture Port Moresby on New Guinea and use it as a springboard to invade Australia. An American battle group intercepted the invasion force in May. For the first time in history, the opposing fleets never came within sight of each other. Aircraft did all the damage.

It was during this battle that Navy aviator Butch O'Hare, flying a Grumman Wildcat, singlehandedly attacked a formation of Japanese bombers closing in on the American fleet. The heavily armored Wildcat withstood a hail of bullets. O'Hare, the namesake of Chicago's O'Hare International Airport, shot down five bombers and damaged a sixth, for which he won the Congressional Medal of Honor.

Later in the war, Marine aviator and Wildcat sharpshooter Joe Foss shot down 27 aircraft during the brutal six-month campaign for Guadalcanal. Throughout its service, the Wildcat proved itself as an incredibly tough fighter.

The Widgeon's war record is less glamorous than that of the fighters, but it was vital in antisubmarine operations and air-sea rescue. *(Photo courtesy of Charles Coppi.)*

In 1945, Plant 2 at Bethpage was in the midst of peak wartime production. Grumman set a number of U.S. production records, including one for the most planes of a single type — the Hellcat shown here — in one month. In March 1945, 605 were built. *(Photo courtesy of the Grumman History Center.)*

Grumman had installed self-sealing fuel tanks and an armored cockpit to protect the pilot, features lacking in the Japanese Zero. It could (and did) take a beating day after day, both in combat and in normal wear and tear, and still remained operational. The Zero, on the other hand, not only sacrificed pilot protection for speed and maneuverability, but was also difficult to maintain in the corrosive jungles of the South Pacific.

The importance of the Wildcat in the Pacific was underscored by James Forrestal, undersecretary of the Navy, who said in 1943, "Grumman saved Guadalcanal."[22] Despite its shortcomings, the Zero was still faster and far more maneuverable than the Wildcat and had greater range. In 1942, Grumman was happy to get hold of an intact Zero. After studying its strengths and defects, the company's engineers in 1943 designed and put into production the F6F Hellcat fighter, which outclassed the Zero in every respect. It soon became the darling of the Navy's aviators. One even went so far as to say, "If the Hellcat could cook, I'd marry it."[23]

Just prior to the attack on Pearl Harbor, Grumman delivered a new torpedo plane to the Navy. Originally designated the TBF, the torpedo plane became known as the "Avenger" after the attack. The Grumman Avenger, like the Wildcat and its successor, the Hellcat, shouldered the burden of the Pacific war.

A Call to Arms

The war shut down all civilian aircraft construction in the rush to fill President Franklin D. Roosevelt's call for the production of 60,000 aircraft of all types in 1942 and even larger orders during 1943 and 1944. The aircraft industry met the challenge in a burst of productivity unmatched in history. At its height, Grumman Aircraft alone employed more than 20,500 workers, supplying most of the fighters and torpedo planes used in the Pacific.[24]

As Richard Thruelson wrote in his comprehensive account of Grumman's history, *The Grumman Story*:

"The unassailable fact is that the people at Grumman did a remarkable job during World War II — especially remarkable in that they adjusted to all the pressures and demands of the wartime economy without losing the spirit, the character, and the homogeneity that had so distinguished the Grumman enterprise in its early years."[25]

The F4F Wildcat fighter descended directly from the FiFi. Rugged and dependable, the Wildcat was slower and less maneuverable than its opponent, the Japanese Zero, but it was heavily armed and armored. In the hands of incredibly brave naval aviators, the airplane helped turn the tide of the Pacific war. *(Photo courtesy of the Grumman History Center.)*

Grumman became known as the Iron Works because of their planes' built-in structural integrity and safety factors, which made the aircraft stronger and heavier than required. In fact, military pilots used to joke that Grumman would have built the aircraft out of concrete, but they always found something heavier.

Sales skyrocketed from $22 million in 1941 to more than $324 million in 1944, although net income increased only slightly. During these years, Grumman won the coveted Army-Navy "E for Excellence" award no less than seven times.

Altogether, Grumman aircraft were reported to have shot down more than 60 percent of the enemy aircraft destroyed in the Pacific.[26] The stubby F4F Wildcat checked the Japanese advance in the Pacific and turned the tide in the first two years of the war. The F6F Hellcat proved to be more than a match for the famed Zero and is credited with destroying about 5,000 enemy aircraft.[27] In a testament to Grumman's success, Vice Admiral John S. McCain said, "The name Grumman is like sterling on silver."[28]

The Concept Begins to Emerge

The end of World War II brought a unique set of challenges. On August 14, 1945, the Japanese accepted

Above: The F6F Hellcat went into production in 1943 and succeeded the Wildcat. Designed with the Zero's performance capabilities in mind, the Hellcat was more than a match for its adversary. *(Photo courtesy of the Grumman History Center.)*

Below: The Army-Navy "E for Excellence" award.

surrender terms following the atomic destruction of Hiroshima and Nagasaki. On August 15, Roy Grumman watched as the federal government canceled 85 percent of its orders in a single day. He knew the day of wartime contracts would come to an end sooner or later. Even before the war, he did not want to rely exclusively on government contracts. The coming peace promised new opportunities in the civilian sector. Now, with the prospect of thousands of young airmen returning, he expected that pilots would not be ready to hang up their flight suits when they reentered civilian life.

This view was backed up by the federal Department of Commerce, which reported to Congress that light planes "represented the most logical field for postwar expansion of the aeronautical industry." Peacetime production was expected to reach 200,000 aircraft per year.[29] Grumman Aircraft began designing several light aircraft models for the aviation

Although Grumman Aircraft was preeminent in the field of naval aviation, Roy Grumman wished to build an airplane for the peaceful occupation of business. The G-73 Mallard was the result. *(Photo courtesy of Charles Coppi.)*

LEROY GRUMMAN:
MORE THAN A MODEST SUCCESS

WHEN LEROY "ROY" Grumman retired in 1966, he had, in the words of one author, "failed to achieve a modest success." He wanted to keep his original Grumman Aircraft Engineering Company small and personalized, but by the time he stepped down, the company's payroll was 33,000-strong and its revenues were over $1 billion.

In his 36 years as its head, Grumman Aircraft had evolved into Grumman Aerospace, its line of products advancing from metal and fabric aircraft capable of 195 miles an hour to jet-powered fighters capable of Mach 2. The year of his departure coincided with the first operation of the lunar excursion module built by Grumman, which would be used to land men on the moon in 1969.[1]

Roy Grumman was born on January 4, 1895, in Huntington, Long Island, the son of George Tyson Grumman, a carriage maker. From the moment flight became a reality, Roy knew his future was in the heavens. Even his salutatorian address to Huntington High School's Class of 1911 was titled "The Aeroplane."

Five years later, he graduated from Cornell University with a degree in engineering and enlisted in the U.S. Navy, where he fulfilled his dream of becoming an aviator when he became naval aviator No. 1216. He then earned his degree in aeronautical engineering from the Massachusetts

boom anticipated by the aircraft industry. The result was the Kitten and the Tadpole, small two- and three-seat all-metal monoplane aircraft developed just before the war ended. Neither went beyond the prototype stage because both would have been overpriced. In any case, the light airplane market failed to take off as expected.

Grumman also produced what has been described by aviation writers as one of the most admired and beautifully designed amphibians ever to fly. The G-73 Mallard featured a luxurious cabin and dressing room, including separate lavatory and baggage compartments. Couches, tables and overstuffed chairs were offered as options. It seated up to 12 passengers and was powered by two 600-horsepower Wasp engines.[30] The cabin even contained thermostatically controlled heating and ventilation.

The prototype Mallard was flown in April 1946. Mallard customers included Vincent Astor, 20th Century Fox and Texaco. While market research indicated at least 250 buyers for the Mallard, the market never materialized, and only 59 were built between 1946 and 1951.[31] Several factors contributed to the lack of interest in the Mallard. The growing number of airfields during this time began to reduce the need for amphibian aircraft. In addition, war surplus aircraft — such as the ubiquitous DC-3 — were readily available.[32]

Roy Grumman still had a warm spot in his heart for civilian aircraft, and there was a growing awareness within the company's higher ranks that there was a need for specifically designed executive transport. "I wouldn't mind building another commercial airplane before I retire," he

---

Institute of Technology. Following transfer to the League Island Naval Yard, near Philadelphia, he served as a test pilot for aircraft built by the Loening Aeronautical Engineering Corporation, a pioneer aviation company started by two brothers, Grover and Albert Loening. It was there that Grumman and four friends — Leon "Jake" Swirbul, Bill Schwendler, Ed Poor and Clint Towl — decided to start an aircraft repair shop to fix the fragile and unreliable Loenings.

Roy Grumman's shy, reserved exterior belied his towering engineering talents. He ran his company in a short-sleeve, open-door, feet-on-the-desk manner. "Roy Grumman just wanted a 5,000-personnel company where everyone could live on Long Island, get a company turkey at Christmas and just be very happy," explained Robert Smyth, retired vice president of flight operations and quality control for Gulfstream Aerospace. "Anything beyond that wasn't what he wanted."[2]

But the company gained a reputation for excellence, and Roy became something of a celebrity. In 1944, *Time* magazine featured a picture of him on the cover with a story called "Planemaker Grumman."

"There is nothing of the big business tycoon about Roy Grumman in his office. As soon as he gets there, he takes off his coat. Then he props his feet on the desk or an open drawer, puts a pipe or cigar in his mouth and is ready to make all the Hellcats the Navy needs."[3]

He was respected by those who worked for and with him. "Mr. Grumman was a quiet, unassuming man. He was not the demanding type of boss. He was confident that you could do the job. He answered his own phone and made his own calls," remembered Lillian Schleicher, Roy Grumman's secretary in the early 1960s.[4]

Grumman relinquished the presidency of Grumman Aircraft in 1946 after a shot of penicillin, administered to fight a case of pneumonia, left him nearly blind. He remained chairman of the company until 1966, when he stepped down and was named chairman emeritus. Although semiretired, he still visited the production lines and attended board meetings. In 1968, he was awarded the first Hunsacker medal from the National Academy of Sciences for his contributions to aeronautical engineering. Leroy Grumman died on October 4, 1982, at the age of 87.

One of the most admired and beautifully designed amphibians ever built, the Mallard debuted in 1946. It sold for $90,000. *(Photo courtesy of the Grumman History Center.)*

reportedly said. "Heck, I'd like to do one rather than keep doing these weapon systems."[33]

"This is where his vision came through," recalled Charles Coppi, retired senior vice president of engineering for Gulfstream, in 1999. "He was convinced that as the world recovered from the rubble of World War II, business was going to gear up, good things were going to happen and commercial air transportation was really going to take off."[34]

It was during the years following WW II that a small group of Grummanites, headed by Charles Coppi and Goldie Glenn, established an overhaul and service center at Bethpage. This group also provided maintenance for the Grumman corporate and demonstrator aircraft. In the beginning, service was limited to the G21, G44, Mallard, Navion and Beechcraft. In 1948, a contract was signed with Scandinavian Airlines to perform turnaround inspections and to introduce phased maintenance, which was the forerunner of the present-day preventative maintenance systems. The service operation continued up until the introduction of the Gulfstream I.

Coppi joined Grumman after graduating from New York University in 1952 with a degree in aeronautical engineering and the Chance Vought Memorial airplane design award. In 1955, after working on the Rigel missile system, Coppi was invited to join the Preliminary Design Department by Joe Gavin, Grumman's chief engineer (later in charge of the lunar excursion module for Project Apollo). Coppi joined other engineers in the "Snake Pit," a windowless area located in the bowels of the Bethpage plant. That invitation and the assignment to the Gulfstream project were the start of a 40-year adventure for Coppi, who played a principal role in conceptual development for all five Gulfstreams. In time, he would be known as "Mr. Gulfstream" for his contributions.

Back in the pit, however, engineers had not bought into Roy Grumman's vision. For a period of time, nothing was done. "The feeling was," recalled Coppi, "'We're here to build war machines for the Navy. Why do we want to fool around with that?' There wasn't any urge to get on with it."[35]

But the era of the corporate aircraft had arrived. American industry was untouched during World War II. It stood ready to supply the needs of a still-devastated world as well as the needs and desires of the average American, armed with a fattened bank account and a seemingly insatiable appetite for consumer goods.

Another factor in favor of a genuine corporate aircraft was also at work. In the forties and fifties, the federal government relaxed its antitrust policies. It was not long before conglomerates rose on the business landscape like skyscrapers, operating factories all over the United States. It became imperative for executive teams to be able to visit their corporations' holdings without relying on the fickle schedules of the major airlines.

As Coppi later noted, "The enormous growth in business, commerce and consumer goods meant that the business communities would require a modern business aircraft to serve the needs of an ever-expanding industrial world. The vision was being focused, and the opportunity to utilize the company's resources to create a unique product was at hand."[36]

Assembly of the first Gulfstreams. Critics predicted few customers for the new business airplane. *(Photo courtesy of Albert Glenn.)*

CHAPTER TWO

BUILDING A LEGACY

1958–1959

"The Gulf Stream current can be characterized as swift, powerful, predictable and dependable. You could count on it — and that is what the Grumman Gulfstream was all about."

— Charles Coppi, 1999[1]

ROY GRUMMAN'S PATIENCE WORE thin as he awaited ideas for a business transport from the Preliminary Design Department. Over a period of weeks, he called down to the Snake Pit to gauge their progress. Getting no result, he called down one more time and said, "Hey, what's going on? I want to see something!"[2]

The group got the message that the front office was serious. "All hell broke loose to come up with some ideas," Charles Coppi remembered.[3] Coppi was one of the first of a very small group that started to look in earnest at what Grumman could do to develop a modern business aircraft.[4] Besides Roy Grumman, the Gulfstream project had a number of fathers and midwives, so to speak. Bill Schwendler, one of the cofounders of Grumman, took the project under his wing and helped push it through to fruition. The engineering effort was headed by Bernie Harriman, who died during the development phase of the Gulfstream II.

One of the most ardent proponents of the challenging commercial project, however, was a nonengineer named Henry Schiebel. A master salesman, Schiebel also piloted the Douglas DC-3s owned by Grumman Aircraft. As both a pilot and a salesman, he kept in close contact with fellow pilots from major corporations because the task of selling what commercial aircraft Grumman offered had fallen to Schiebel in the days of the Widgeon and the Mallard. Consequently, he was familiar with both the popularity and the limitations of the DC-3, the most widely used transport at the time. The DC-3 was a sturdy aircraft that well deserved its reputation for reliability. In its day, the DC-3 was unrivaled as a passenger plane. At an average price tag of just $200,000, the DC-3 demonstrated with great clarity that flying could be safe, reliable, affordable and economical.

However, the airplane had a top speed of just 160 knots, and it struggled against headwinds. Furthermore, the unpressurized cabin was not very comfortable, keeping the aircraft from flying above 8,000 feet. That meant it had to fly through, rather than above, bad weather, subjecting the aircraft and its passengers to violent buffeting that churned even the strongest stomachs. In the summer, the cabin was an oven; in the winter, an icebox.

Early in the design phase, Roy Grumman wanted to keep costs down by converting an existing aircraft design into a business transport. Grumman engineers first looked at the S2F-1 Tracker, a high-wing Navy antisubmarine

Early Gulfstream designs were usually built as desktop models. This is the final design for the Gulfstream I. *(Photo courtesy of the Grumman History Center.)*

An early design brochure for Design 159, which would become the Gulfstream I. Engineers initially considered adapting Grumman's S2F-1 Tracker, a relatively slow, high-wing antisubmarine airplane, but that would have defeated the purpose of marketing an airplane for business use. *(Photo courtesy of Herman Schonenberg.)*

search aircraft, as a cost-efficient answer. Its conversion would be accomplished by retaining the wing and tail and adding turbine engines and a pressurized fuselage.[5]

But the idea of using the Tracker was, in fact, the antithesis of what they wanted to accomplish. The Tracker was built for the purpose of flying low and slow, the kind of performance expected from a good subkiller but clearly not the attributes of a corporate aircraft.[6] Engineers kept tinkering with the idea, trying to get it to fit within the specifications without totally abandoning the Tracker's basic design.

Meanwhile, as the engineers worked, Henry Schiebel enlisted the help of engineer Peter Viemeister and visited the potential customers of Design 159, so designated because it was the next design number available, to see what they really wanted.

Conceiving the 159

Schiebel and Viemeister developed a questionnaire and went to work. "We tried to find out things like what airports they visited," Viemeister recalled in 1999. "We asked, are they always big hub airports or do executives need to go to little airports? What kind of runway length do they want to be able to operate from?" They also asked what sort of cost and creature comforts were expected from an aircraft with a potential price tag of $1 million, whether they preferred high-wing or low-wing configuration, and what sort of engine they felt comfortable with.[7]

Thus began a longstanding practice in the development of future Gulfstream aircraft to canvass prospective customers so their requirements could be included in the development and design of the aircraft. Among those who came to critique the evolution of the Gulfstream were Nelson Rokes of Procter & Gamble, Don Baldwin of Texaco, Steve Brown of Continental Can, Harold Curtis of National Distillers, Jim Hopkins of American Can, Bill Shaughnessey of American Cyanamid and Charlie Morris of Mobil.[8]

A new fuselage was adopted, but engineers hoped to keep the Tracker's basic wing planform and empennage design. As Schiebel reported the results of his surveys, however, engineers realized they had to start with a clean sheet of paper. "Roy Grumman was kind of grimacing, like 'Just do a whole new airplane,'" said Viemeister. They concluded that they should be designing a miniature airliner.

There was still a debate over whether to retain the high wing or go with a low wing, and two engineering groups went head-to-head in an all-out competition to determine the right configuration. Coppi had the enviable assignment of putting together the low-wing design as part of the team of true believers. The low-wingers, buttressed by the weight of Schiebel's surveys, won out in the end. Schiebel and Viemeister noted that pilots and passengers alike felt more secure with a low-wing model. Among the reasons: Passengers liked the feeling that they were riding on a platform rather than hanging from a wing. From the pilots' point of view, they felt they had a better view with a low wing. They also knew — some from first-hand experience as Navy pilots in World War II — that if they had to ditch in the sea, they stood a better chance of surviving with a low wing.

The competition took weeks but the decision itself took only a few minutes. After the competing groups presented their cases, Roy Grumman, smoking his ever-present pipe, simply said, "Low wing."[9]

One prospective customer request, for ample passenger visibility, led to a Gulfstream design trademark. Grumman executives came up with the idea of installing large elliptical windows.[10] The windows, which were installed on the first Gulfstream, have appeared on every Gulfstream aircraft produced since.

The windows dictated a fair amount of the design of the fuselage, recalled George Viteritti, an engineer in the 159's Structural Design Group.

"To put an exit around that big window, you'd end up with a huge door.... We put together a proposal that went to the FAA and told them that we felt our window was equivalent to the FAA escape hatch that was required. So they had us do a test, which we did. And we showed we could evacuate the airplane with a cross section of people. As a result, two windows over the wing became hatches."[11]

Jet versus Turboprop

Deciding on the type of power plant to adopt was, by comparison, one of the easier decisions made by Grumman. Engineers briefly considered (then quickly abandoned) the thought of using jet engines. Instead, they favored turboprops for this first business aircraft, even though jet power was being introduced into rival aircraft such as the Lockheed JetStar and North American's Sabreliner. The teething problems associated with this still relatively new propulsion system were just too numerous, especially with the risks Grumman was already taking.

Jet engines at that time consumed a great amount of fuel, which reduced their effective range. Although faster than turboprops, jets ate up the extra time gained in the air with frequent fuel stops. They also required longer runways for takeoff and landing, making a jet impractical for businessmen with holdings in out-of-the-way places. To power an aircraft the size envisioned by Roy Grumman, furthermore, would have required four jet engines, each of which required a higher degree of maintenance than turboprops.

There was a final reason for staying away from jet engines, as Charles Coppi explained:

"The thinking was that as the Air Force and Navy downsized, a lot of military pilots would be coming out and finding their way into business aviation departments. Those guys were piston jockeys, and the transition from piston to turboprop was a lot easier, a lot more forgiving, and gave them a lot more confidence than going from a piston engine right into jet operation."[12]

Some of the prime criteria for the product philosophy of the 159 program were reliability, dependability, safety and experience. So when engineers looked around for the right turboprop, they decided on the Rolls-Royce Dart, which powered the British-made Vickers Viscount. The Dart had more than a million hours of service behind it, so its track record as a safe and reliable engine was undeniable. And as an added bonus, the original engine nacelles fit into the design nicely, allowing passengers to look out and see the double RR, a powerful symbol of both prestige and the reputation of a proven engine manufacturer.

The advantages of the Dart over jet engines and other turboprops were explained by engineers Coppi, Lawrence Mead and John Strakosch in a case study prepared for the American Institute of Aeronautics and Astronautics (AIAA) that compared the development programs of the first three Gulfstreams:

"[The Dart] already had an impressive reliability record. Although we knew that the pure jet would be competition and some were already flying, the turboprop would give much more range for a given size and would make bad weather holding patterns less worrisome to the pilots. Range was set by consideration of what would be a reasonable, maximum one-day flight, six to eight hours. At Gulfstream I cruising speeds this meant a maximum range of 2,500 statute miles, permitting flights to anywhere in the world, in reasonable stage lengths."[13]

The importance of reliability didn't end with the engines. Every part of the aircraft was to exude strength and foster a feeling of confidence, right down to the stairway. Bill Schwendler insisted on a sturdy, self-contained stairway in the aircraft. "The first thing people see when they go into this aircraft is the stairs," he told engineers. "You have

This is an early rendition of the Gulfstream I's paint scheme. The prototype GI was painted in these colors, but production models were delivered as unfinished "greenies." *(Image courtesy of the Grumman History Center.)*

to make the stairs tough and husky so they feel confident that it is really built well."[14]

First Flight

As Design 159 progressed, another critical decision was needed — what to name the new airplane. After rejecting several names, Roy Grumman suggested calling the 159 the "Gulfstream" because many of Grumman's executives enjoyed vacationing in Florida, where the Gulf Stream (it is two words when referring to the current) runs off the coast and flows northward. "The name clearly conveyed a touch of class and distinction in the promotion of the aircraft.... The Gulf Stream current can be characterized as swift, powerful, predictable and dependable. You could count on it — and that is what the Grumman Gulfstream was all about. But the name Gulfstream went beyond the visible product identification. It characterized Grumman's fundamental design philosophy for the aircraft," explained Coppi.[15]

In July 1958, all Grumman employees were introduced to the company's latest product. An article in the *Grumman Plane News* stated that the Gulfstream had a maximum speed of 350 miles an hour at 25,000 feet and a range of 2,200 miles and could achieve a maximum altitude of 33,600 feet. The cabin had comfortable seating for up to 12 passengers and somewhat more cramped accommodations for up to 24 if the need arose, in addition to two crew members. The lavatory had hot and cold running water. A fully loaded Gulfstream was capable of taking off and landing from runways under 4,000 feet, though Federal Aviation Administration (FAA) regulations required a takeoff field length of 4,350 feet and a landing field of 4,000 feet.[16] Furthermore, the aircraft could operate independent of ground support. An auxiliary power unit could keep the instruments and climate control operating while on the ground, and the stairway was operated hydraulically.

Engineers had achieved their goal: the aircraft resembled a small passenger liner, with a wing span of 78 feet 6 inches and an overall length of 63 feet 9 inches. The cabin itself was 33 feet long and almost 7.5 feet wide, with a ceiling height of just over 6 feet.

A fuel truck fills the GI for its maiden flight. The airplane was airborne for only a few minutes before mechanical trouble forced the pilots to return. *(Photo courtesy of Bob Smyth.)*

The Gulfstream was ready for its first flight. Even before it took to the air, however, skeptics predicted the program was destined to fail. At $845,000, the initial price tag for a Gulfstream, the naysayers believed that the aircraft was priced far out of range for the market. Some even felt that there simply was no market for a corporate airplane like the Gulfstream.[17]

Other publications, such as *Flight* magazine, questioned Grumman's choice of engines. "Will the straight jet or the propjet be the most popular in the new family of high performance business air transports now in the works? Grumman Aircraft Engineering Corporation believes the propjet will take the honors."[18] Undaunted by its critics, Grumman pressed ahead, and on August 14, 1958, Carl Alber and Fred Rowley made the first test flight of the Gulfstream, with Grumman pilot Bob Smyth flying in a chase plane to observe the aircraft's performance and lend assistance, if needed. As the Gulfstream ascended, Smyth pulled up next to Alber and Rowley.[19] He immediately saw that both men were holding their noses, pointing to their headsets and giving thumbs down — the signal that something was wrong with the aircraft and their radios were out. The air-

Although mechanical trouble forced the GI to land prematurely, the pilots performed all the necessary maneuvers for this to count as the Gulfstream's first flight. *(Photo courtesy of the Grumman History Center.)*

craft had lost all electrical power. And then the right engine suddenly quit when they reached about 800 feet. The pilots feathered the right-hand propeller to reduce drag and then returned to land as quickly as possible.

On the ground, a member of the National Business Aviation Association was on hand to witness the first flight. Standing next to him was Henry Schiebel. As the Gulfstream approached for a landing, Schiebel, ever the salesman, exclaimed, "Look at that single engine performance!" Rowley and Alber alighted from the plane calmly and said, "This thing handles beautifully."[20]

Technically, the flight was a success because the pilots took off, performed a 180 degree turn, and then landed. "First flights are successful if you land and nothing else happens," Smyth said in a 1999 interview.[21] Reminiscing about the flight, Smyth explained what happened. Essentially, systems meant to power the aircraft in flight were somehow wired to a "weight on wheels" switch that controlled the "on/off" for items meant to be used on the ground. When the aircraft took off, the power to the

Above: Bob Smyth flew the F8F Bearcat chase plane during the GI's first flight, which was piloted by Carl Alber and Fred Rowley. (Photo courtesy of Bob Smyth.)

Left: Grumman test pilots Alber and Rowley (left to right) landed the GI on one engine. As they landed, that engine quit as well. (Photo courtesy of the Grumman History Center.)

in-flight electronics was cut off. When that happened, the electric fuel-boost pumps lost power.[22]

That by itself was not enough to cut off the engines, Smyth said. "You can get along up to 15,000 or 20,000 feet without the boost pump on, if everything is working normally," he explained.

"But, and I know this for a fact, during the checkout phase a little O-ring was lost in the fuel system. Well, they couldn't find it, so they put another O-ring in and put the pump back together.

Well, this little O-ring worked its way against the filter. When the pilots reduced rpm, with the pump off and the fuel being squeezed off by this little O-ring, it quit."[23]

The engineers ironed out the problems, and the aircraft underwent about 800 hours of flight test time. On May 21, 1959, the Gulfstream received FAA certification, and the first Gulfstream was soon delivered to Sinclair Oil. Henry Schiebel managed sales in conjunction with four distributors, who were responsible for adding the avionics and the interiors. This arrangement allowed customers to personalize their aircraft by working with the distributor rather than directly with Grumman, a practice the company learned the hard way after its experience with the Mallard, noted Peter Viemeister.

"The front office said, 'You know, when we did Mallards, we'd sell to Mr. Big Shot, but then we'd have to deal with Mrs. Big Shot, who wanted leopard skin and green carpet and purple curtains. Then we'd do the curtains, and she'd say, 'I don't like that. Take it out.' The Grumman guys said, 'We don't want to get into the interior decorating business. We build airplanes. We're not even going to paint them, just zinc chromate them and let the distributor handle the rest."[24]

This approach was not popular with Albert "Goldie" Glenn and others, who envisioned a whole new product line and an additional means of tying the customers into the manufacturer for future business.

From the beginning, Grumman flew "greenies," as they were called because of the green zinc chromate coating, to distributors to customize. Grummanites proudly declared their newest aircraft as perfect "for the leaders of industry to whom time is priceless." But it wasn't only corporations that were interested in the Gulfstream. TV personality Arthur Godfrey, for instance, inquired about purchasing a Gulfstream. Schiebel was leery of allowing sales to famous entertainers because he didn't trust them to fly the airplanes safely and responsibly. Like a father, he worried about preserving the aircraft's good name. (Godfrey did purchase a Gulfstream eventually, from National Financing Corporation in 1967.)[25]

A New Breed

While the Gulfstream was still under development, Albert "Goldie" Glenn realized that "we can't just put airplanes out there. We were very keenly aware of the need to support these aircraft, and I was in charge of technical support."[26] Glenn knew he faced an uphill battle because the thought of providing full support for aircraft back then was abhorrent to most of the industry; designated distributors filled that role, leaving the manufacturer free to keep turning out aircraft. The proposal that Grumman fully support its Gulfstream program touched off controversy within the company.

The Gulfstream I was sought after by corporations, entertainers and actors, but Grumman was leery of selling to the latter two categories. *(Photo courtesy of the Grumman History Center.)*

Glenn, who eventually rose to become president of Gulfstream, insisted that Grumman had to be the pioneer in the field of support because he recalled how he struggled to get the parts and support to keep the company's DC-3s running. The idea of leaving it to distributors to take care of a plane as unique as the Gulfstream chilled him. Others within the department agreed. Herman "Schoney" Schonenberg, who worked in materials support and sales for the Gulfstream I, explained that it was almost impossible to persuade distributors to stock a reasonable amount of inventory parts. They preferred to come back to Grumman as often as necessary on an "as-needed" basis. "It got to the point where we had to have a meeting, which I attended, where we challenged the officers of the company," Schonenberg said.

"We understood their feeling that they didn't want to get involved in the service end of the business, but the distributors weren't doing their part. They preferred to install the interiors and move out the aircraft. If they needed something, they would come to us on an emergency basis, and we would sell them an emergency part in the middle of the night. We told the officers of our company that the only way the customer is going to be satisfied with the supply and service system is if we do it ourselves."[27]

"We were the first people in manufacturing who were doing full-scale support," added Goldie Glenn. "When I say full-scale support, we were putting out not only maintenance manuals but parts manuals and flight manuals, and we also started the training. In addition, we established maintenance programs to satisfy customer needs."[28] That was the beginning of the long-running relationship with FlightSafety, founded by Al Ueltschi in 1951. Now owned by Berkshire Hathaway, the famous investment firm run by Warren Buffet, FlightSafety was the first company dedicated to improving the skills of pilots.

Glenn recalled that most of Grumman "hated us" for pushing the service center. After some struggle, people behind this effort were able to get their point across. Soon, Grumman was shipping parts to customers all over the country, often within 24 hours. The company was situated close to Kennedy Airport, which made it easy to get the parts out.[29]

In addition to being guaranteed parts, customers also had the advantage of a field representative who stayed with the new operator for a period of time. The field rep took the Gulfstream through its outfitting to make sure the distributor did what it was supposed to do without harming the aircraft's safety and reliability.[30]

While it generated sales and a reputation for outstanding support for the Gulfstream, this new way of supporting aircraft caused some consternation for competitors. Schonenberg remembered sitting at an industry breakfast meeting when the head of sales for one of Gulfstream's competitors came up to him and said, "You son-of-a-bitch. You set up a program so tough that we can't meet you."[31]

The Gulfstream was the culmination of Roy Grumman's dream of getting into the civilian aviation market. Although Grumman's bread and butter would continue to come from military sales, the company had a first-of-its-kind, world-class business aircraft unlike anything then flying. Pilots who flew the Gulfstream I have said it was perfect for its job as executive transport. Its interior comfort was matched with smooth handling that was forgiving. It was heavy in the air, which meant that pilots and passengers were not subjected to sudden jerking motions common to lighter aircraft.

A Tide of Gulfstreams

Far from losing its shirt, as critics predicted, Grumman sold 200 Gulfstreams over the course of the aircraft's 11-year production life to such prestigious companies as Sinclair Oil, Owens-Corning Fiberglas Corporation, Texaco, Dow Chemical, the Upjohn Company, United States Steel, Martin Marietta, Brown & Root, the Columbia Broadcasting System (CBS), and Walt Disney. Even the FAA bought a pair.

In 1966, the U.S. Navy purchased nine Gulfstreams to be used as bombardier/navigation training aircraft. Designated the TC-4C Academe, the airplane had a cabin outfitted as a simulated A-6 Intruder cockpit, complete with the Intruder's electronic navigation attack system, as well as four bombardier/navigation consoles.

In his account of the Gulfstream I program, author Richard Thruelson noted that, though a great deal can be said for its comfort and versatility, "its most noteworthy characteristic was, and is, its reliability. Its design and construction made it virtually a failsafe airplane.... This sort of safety record doesn't just happen; it is earned by good piloting, sound design, conscientious construction, and proper maintenance."[32]

The Gulfstream I Today: Still Flying

In 1998 the first Gulfstream celebrated its 40th birthday. At the time, serial number 001 was still in operation in South Africa and was owned and operated through a partnership between Vanellus Air and RossAir Executive Air Charter Operations.[33] The Gulfstream was making three- to four-hour daily flights from South Africa's Wonderboom municipal airport, located outside the capital of Pretoria, to a variety of destinations, including Namibia, Zimbabwe, Zambia and Mozambique.[34]

The aircraft is also used on longer two- to three-day excursions to Ethiopia, Sudan, Nigeria and Ghana.[35] The 12-seat GI is used primarily for transporting business people and government officials. It had also played an important role in helping to evacuate casualties from South African war zones to Johannesburg for care.

In the 1960s, when Grumman was selected by NASA to produce the Lunar Space Module, the first Gulfstream was fitted with a cargo door to help transport some of the pieces that were to be used in the lunar module, which would carry astronauts Neil Armstrong and Ed "Buzz" Aldrin to the moon.[36] In 1998, this particular cargo door had a much different use. Vanellus Air was using the Gulfstream I to transport sick and injured people throughout Africa to cities where medical care was available. The cargo door made it easier to get casualties on board.[37]

Johan S. Marais, Aviation Manager for Vanellus Air, summed up what it was like working with the first Gulfstream as it approached its 40th birthday.

"Taking into consideration that this aircraft is 40 years old and the type of work that we still do with this aircraft [and that] Africa is not an easy place in which to operate, ... the fact that we can do it with this aircraft is remarkable. And we do it in fairly good comfort and style."[38]

This is the first Gulfstream on its 40th anniversary in 1998. At the time, it was being operated daily by Vanellus Air, a South African charter service. *(Photo courtesy of Gulfstream Aerospace.)*

In 1967, the Gulfstream program moved to Savannah, Georgia. Shown here is the GII production line. *(Photo courtesy of Albert Glenn.)*

CHAPTER THREE

DEPARTURES

1960–1969

"It was the most successful first flight we ever had. Flawless. There were no problems at all."

— GII Test Pilot Carl Alber, 1966[1]

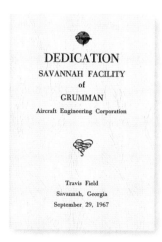

DEDICATION

SAVANNAH FACILITY
of
GRUMMAN
Aircraft Engineering Corporation

Travis Field
Savannah, Georgia
September 29, 1967

I N EARLY 1963, A SMALL 8-FOOT BY 14-foot room, just big enough for two people and two drafting tables, was set aside away from the Gulfstream program's main project area. Here, Charles Coppi and an apprentice began the design work on a jet-powered Gulfstream.[2] The room itself was off the main project area for several reasons. "First of all, it kept things kind of quiet because you didn't want stuff leaking out and upsetting the Gulfstream I sales effort," remembered Coppi, who was the lead engineer for the GII project. "Second thing, there was a little air of mystery. Customers did find out that something was going on; they just didn't know exactly what."[3]

The first Gulfstream was a breakthrough in business aviation, and Grumman was delivering an average of about two per month to customers ranging from the U.S. military to the Swiss post office. Grumman adopted a policy of continual product improvement and development from the beginning of the program, and over the years a number of improvements were made. Maximum payload increased from 4,570 pounds to more than 6,000 pounds. Extra fuel cells were installed, helping to boost the range to more than 2,400 miles. The Gulfstream I overcame the odds, and more than 200 were eventually delivered.

But by the mid-1960s, jet power had emerged as the winner in the debate over jets versus turboprops.

Lockheed JetStars, Dassault Falcons and North American Sabreliners were appearing on the market in ever-increasing numbers. The market was beginning to pay for a jet aircraft's fast, quiet and smooth flight, and the improvements in jet technology over the years made it the next logical step for Grumman.[4] Work on a jet-powered Gulfstream actually began in 1960, but early designs attempting to adapt the GI airframe to jet engines were not successful.

One idea was to match four General Electric CF700 engines to a modified Gulfstream I with its wings swept back by 20 degrees. The design was proposed to Juan Trippe, one of the founders of Pan Am. Trippe was reportedly trying to organize the original "rent-a-plane" program by leasing Lockheed JetStars to companies. Perceiving this a threat to the Gulfstream's market share, Bill Schwendler had a design quickly drawn up that adapted the Gulfstream I to jet power. It wasn't an elegant solution. The aircraft would have flown as far as a JetStar but would have been much slower and was unquestionably nowhere near as attractive. The idea was dropped.[5]

The Savannah plant was dedicated on September 29, 1967. The plant could accommodate two production lines. *(Photo courtesy of the Grumman History Center.)*

From the start of the GII program, designated the G.1159, engineers knew what sort of performance they were looking for. Grumman intended to keep all of the attributes that made the first Gulfstream a success — safety, reliability, comfort and confidence — and add the advantages of jet-age technologies for speed, performance, range and high altitudes afforded by the power and smoothness of jet engines. The challenge was finding the right engine.

Guiding that selection process, as well as the configuration definition, was a product design philosophy that was unique in the business aircraft community. The dominant features of that philosophy were proven airline-quality engines with power to spare; conservative wing sizing for a generous flight envelope and well-behaved flight characteristics; a wing big enough to house all of the mission fuel for safety, plus reserve tankage for growth; evolutionary design principles blended with technology advances that produced a payback to the operator in terms of operating efficiencies; and a robust and dependable airframe with a long service life.

As Coppi noted, "These principles focused on Grumman's time-tested philosophy — that whatever you do, do it well and make sure it's technically better than anything in the market."[6]

No Limits

As the preliminary design process grew, the design team began incorporating the key features gleaned from frequent contacts with Gulfstream customers. These contacts, encouraged by Coppi and Henry Schiebel, the master salesman/pilot who pushed for the project from the beginning, became formalized as annual Maintenance Symposiums, in which pilots and passengers, mechanics and maintenance staffs were invited to air opinions on all aspects of their Gulfstreams. These meetings continued into the next century in the form of customer review boards and an annual workshop.

"We took all the recognized maintenance issues and brought them out on the floor," explained Herman Schonenberg, the maintenance manager for the Gulfstream at the time. "Our engineering department would be on hand to listen to all the criticisms. The engineering people would say exactly what we were going to do about it. Then we would open the meeting up to anyone else. In the end, the customer felt we were really listening to him and trying to address his concerns."[7]

When the first Gulfstream project was launched, engineers had operated within set boundaries. They knew it would be a twin turboprop of some type with straight wings and a comfortable cabin. The GII, on the other hand, began with just one boundary: The

---

When designing its new aircraft, Gulfstream considered several powerplants but finally decided to stick with Rolls-Royce and its Spey Mark 511 jet engine. The new engine produced 11,400 pounds of thrust.

basic cross-section of the aircraft and the overall length would remain relatively intact so that the new aircraft would not give up any usable cabin volume.

The emphasis on jet power addressed the two most important items that customers wanted: greater speed and range. The GII had to have the ability to fly between any two airports within the continental United States. That meant nonstop flights from New York to Los Angeles or Miami to Seattle against 80-knot to 90-knot headwinds.[8] But it also had to retain the ability to get in and out of relatively short runways of under 6,000 feet, which comprised the bulk of the world's airports. In addition, the aircraft needed to have the ability to fly at 43,000 feet, high enough to get over airline traffic, and have a maximum cruising speed in the Mach .8 range. "In short," noted aviation authors Steve Saunders and I.A. Woodhouse, "it had to be one hell of an aeroplane!"[9]

The Nucleus of the GII: Jet Power

At one time or another, seven different types of engines were considered during the conceptual phase of the GII. General Electric, Lycoming, and Pratt & Whitney all contended for the prestige of powering the second Gulfstream, but ultimately Grumman stayed with Rolls-Royce, picking the Spey Mark 511, a powerful engine that put out 11,400 pounds of thrust.[10] Coppi said the project's philosophy was, "If you want power, we'll give you power to spare."

This statement was the hallmark of every Gulfstream. "The Spey 511 had everything a customer wanted to fit that philosophy," he said.

"We picked it because it fit our product design criteria and it had a proven production heritage in

Choosing an engine for the GII was not easy. Engineers debated whether to use four smaller engines (two shown on the left side of the model above) or two larger ones (one shown on the right). *(Photo courtesy of Gulfstream Aerospace.)*

several British civil airliners. Further, it was a low-bypass-ratio turbofan, which was a slight upgrade from a pure turbojet. It was a powerful engine for its time with great cruise efficiency and power at the high altitudes we were designing for.... The size of the core engine relative to the size of the fan made it a real sparkling performer at altitudes above airline traffic. The Spey allowed us to do that, while all other engines sort of pooped out."[11]

Smaller engines tended to lose thrust at higher altitudes, forcing pilots to throttle all the way forward to the maximum cruise power settings. The Spey, on the other hand, provided a comfortable margin to maximum cruise power, which meant pilots had more power to fall back on in an emergency.

Furthermore, the Spey 511 was the second generation of Rolls-Royce turbofan engines and had racked up thousands of hours on airliners and combat aircraft. This gave Gulfstream a solidly accurate prediction of the engine's maintenance requirements and costs. In addition, the support system for the 511 was well established.

The engine's overhaul life was a substantial 7,000 hours, and it was lauded as one of the most reliable turbofan engines ever built.[12]

One of the engine's drawbacks, however, was its noise, a factor that would eventually have an enormous impact on the aviation industry. To counteract the noise in the cabin, the twin Speys were mounted on opposite sides of the rear of the fuselage.

Mounting the engines this way kept the wing clean and made the engines easier to maintain. In fact, the entire GII was being designed to make maintenance easier because the original Gulfstream suffered from military aircraft thinking. Engineers had put performance over ease of access, stuffing equipment in any available space with little regard for convenience. This was an issue that surfaced at the Maintenance Symposiums. Engineers soon learned that "access" and "maintainability" were important words. "The good news, though, was the fact that we did get everything into the rear access

This early artist's conception of the GII highlights the fact that the jet version of the Gulfstream could operate on the same runway as the GI. Note the GI in the background. *(Image courtesy of the Grumman History Center.)*

compartment, nicknamed the 'hell hole.' The bad news was we got everything in one very small compartment," said Goldie Glenn.

"When we built the Gulfstream I, we didn't go through the machinations of a maintenance review as much as we should have," acknowledged Schonenberg.[13]

During the GII design stage, complete mock-ups were built for the first time, using plywood, balsa and metal frames. The mock-ups permitted maintenance personnel and instructors to go over every nut and bolt to determine the maintainability of the aircraft. The mock-ups saved time and money by identifying problem areas before any metal was cut for a prototype. "I think we straightened out an awful lot of things that engineers wouldn't have seen in the maintenance end of the program," Schonenberg added.[14] In addition, potential customers were able to provide crucial suggestions, many of which were included in the design.

The mock-ups served another purpose: Field service representatives, under the control of Roger Wolf Kahn, trained on the mock-ups. The idea of a field service representative, Kahn's brainchild, began on the GI and carried over to the GII. A customer not only bought the aircraft but, for a period of time, received a fully qualified service rep who would accompany the aircraft through outfitting at the distributor, keeping a careful eye on any changes to the aircraft to make sure work was done properly. Reps even traveled to Europe with the operators.[15]

For the GII, a good number of equipment components were installed in the aft section of the fuselage in the wheel well and in the nose wheel, places to which mechanics and service people had easy access. The GII was designed to be able to use the same runway as the GI. It also had a modest wing sweep of about 25 degrees, which made it faster while retaining all the comfort of the original design. In fact, the entire forward section of the GI, including the cockpit, entranceway and electronics rack, was used as the GII's front end.[16] This helped save on retooling and redesign costs.[17]

Like the GI, the GII would be able to operate independent of ground support, with an auxiliary power unit to provide the power to start engines and maintain comfortable cabin temperatures. The trademark stairway was included in the design as well.

In the middle of the project, the management team, which included Bill Schwendler and Clint Towl, two of Grumman's highest officers, met to go over particulars of the aircraft's design. Henry Schiebel was also present. After going around the table, they came to Schiebel, who, though not an engineer, was a man whose opinion carried a lot of weight. Asked what he thought, he said simply, "Airplane doesn't have enough fuel." With so much of the aircraft already designed, the comment had the effect of a grenade thrown on the middle of the table.[18]

Schiebel patiently explained that the National Business Aviation Association (NBAA) had recently introduced a new, more realistic format to measure the range of competing aircraft. The intent was to cut down on "brochuremanship," in which brochures wildly bragged that aircraft seemingly had enough range to fly to the moon. As a result of Schiebel's bombshell, the wing was redesigned to carry more fuel, increasing the range from 2,200 miles — which was actually less than the GI at that point — to 2,700 miles. The Gulfstream II was the first large business aircraft to be designed around the NBAA format.

The T-Tail Controversy

More bombshells were waiting for Coppi and his team of engineers. When the JetStar and Sabreliner began flying, it was soon discovered that the high velocity exhaust caused fatigue damage to the horizontal tail. Grumman engineers, therefore, decided to adopt the "T"-tail, similar to that of the famed Boeing 727 jetliner. The design work was proceeding well, and several wind tunnel tests showed that engineers were on the right track. Then *Aviation Week & Space Technology*, the leading aeronautical magazine, published an article that stopped the program in its tracks. The leading article stated that "Boeing will never build another T-tail airplane."

Project managers Bernie Harriman (left) and Fred Eckert review a model of the GII in 1965. *(Photo courtesy of the Grumman History Center.)*

In certain areas of Grumman, the magazine *Aviation Week* was like a supplemental airplane design manual. Its words carried tremendous weight. The Engineering Department held frantic meetings to discuss the article's impact.[19] If Boeing felt the T design was not a good idea, ran the argument within Grumman, maybe it wasn't a good idea for Gulfstream. The article, in fact, was actually announcing the design of the 737, with which Boeing hoped to serve the regional airliner market. The 737 has a conventional tail built around the existing fuselage cross section of the Boeing 707 and 727.

The T-tail had had its share of deep-stall issues and incidents in the industry, but those had been put to rest by the time engineers began conceiving the GII. Nevertheless, the debate over the T-tail raged for more than three months. With the project on hold, engineers conducted wind tunnel test after wind tunnel test with the conventional tail position. The original problem — damage to the tail from engine exhaust — was confirmed, so a suggestion was made to hang the engines from the wing. That proposal also didn't work; there was a very real prospect of foreign object damage because the powerful Spey engines would act like a powerful vacuum cleaner on dirty runways. Added to that serious issue was one of comfort; those engines would have to be located next to the passenger compartment. Coppi and his team said that in the final analysis, the T-tail arrangement made for a safer and much more efficient aircraft.[20]

Another meeting was held to make a final decision. After listening once again to the pros and cons, Bill Schwendler thought for a few minutes and said they would stick with the T-tail. He also told all those who had misgivings about the tail not to show up at any more meetings. He then told engineers to "go out and find out everything there is to know about T-tail aft-mounted engine designs." Grumman engineers visited DeHavilland, British Aerospace, McDonnell Douglas, Rolls-Royce and, of course, Boeing, where the controversy had its start. They learned that there was a direct correlation between the span of the horizontal part of the tail that forms the "T" and the span across the engine nacelles and fuselage that affected the attitude of the aircraft. In a stall, a T-tail could be buried in "dirty air," the jumbled airflow coming off the wing that can cause a stall so deep the aircraft cannot recover.[21] They learned that they had to move the tail back far enough to ensure good air flow. As the aircraft continued to develop, detailed specifications and performance guarantees were eventually circulated to prospective customers. Grumman's marketing department trumpeted the arrival of the newest corporate aircraft with performance specifications that were heads above the competition.[22] Brochures noted that the "continuing expansion of the world's great businesses, both here and abroad, has demonstrated the need for a corporate jet transport that can bring outlying facilities within easy reach.

"Powered by Rolls-Royce Spey engines, the Gulfstream II is the product of extensive design experience, careful market observations and an appreciation for the needs of the corporate operator. When coupled with its growth potential and the structural integrity inherent in all Grumman products, the aircraft becomes a sound, long-term business investment. Indeed, this combination of design features, plus the most advanced turbofan engine available, ensures Gulfstream II operators of unsurpassed performance for many years."[23]

Incredibly, the production schedule called for the first GII to be built in just over a year. The go-ahead was given in May 1965. By March 1966, half of the fuselage of the first aircraft was already built, and construction had started on a second GII. By the end of that summer, the first aircraft was finished and several "jump-off" tests were conducted. An FAA requirement, jump-offs meant the aircraft could leave the ground for 5, 10 or 15 feet without incidents such as the engine failure that had occurred during the GI's first flight. The FAA made Grumman do 15 jump-offs before allowing the GII to depart from Bethpage.

Bob Smyth, who flew the chase plane during the first flight of the GI, was the test pilot assigned to the GII and conducted the jump-off tests. For the jump-off test, the aircraft is relatively light. It carried only about an hour's worth of fuel because the airplane is not supposed to actually fly, only go down the runway at full power and jump off.

As Smyth ran up the power at the end of the runway, the aircraft was skittering around, wanting to go. "I've had softer catapult shots," he observed.[24] The aircraft jumped off the runway and went airborne, reaching 30 feet as it sailed past the control tower. He was able to wrestle control back from the aircraft and forced it down. "My leg muscles were jumping," admitted Smyth, "from the anxiety."[25]

The aircraft was so light and the Spey engines so powerful that when Smyth powered up for the jump-off, the aircraft nearly took off. A few corrections were made and several more jump-offs conducted without incident, and then the GII was ready for its first flight.

From Drawing Boards to the Skies

On October 2, 1966, less than a year and a half after the go-ahead was given to build the Gulfstream II, the first flight took place. The skies above Bethpage were clear that Sunday afternoon when Smyth and Carl Alber climbed aboard N801G. s/n 0001.[26]

The blue and white Gulfstream II took off at 3:11 p.m. and climbed steeply before leveling off at 10,000 feet above Long Island Sound.[27] "It was tough to hold her back," Smyth later recalled about the flight. "It felt like she really wanted to move out."[28]

About halfway through the flight the automatic pilot was engaged. It was the first time an autopilot was put into operation during a first flight of a corporate aircraft.[29] The flight lasted a total of 52 minutes and was completed when the aircraft landed at Grumman's flight test facility at Calverton in eastern Long Island, about 40 miles away from Bethpage.[30]

"Bob and I worked as a team many times in the past," pilot Carl Alber would say later, "but nothing went any smoother than the first flight of the Gulfstream II. It was a perfect flight."[31]

The No. 1 GII was subsequently flown through its entire speed and altitude envelope, which included stringent tests to excite any flutter tendency. It passed with flying colors.

One of the reasons for the aircraft's success was the "iron monster."[32] This flight control system simulator duplicated the control system of the Gulfstream II in every respect so that the system could be "flown" beforehand to accurately predict the aircraft's flight characteristics.[33]

But when the No. 2 GII was flown in January 1967, the tests didn't go quite as smoothly. At about 28,000 feet on the climb schedule of Mach .75, the pilots began to pick up what they deemed to be an engine vibration. "We assumed it was an engine vibration because it normally went away when either of the engines was throttled back, sometimes both," Smyth said.

"We tried various solutions, including swapping fuel controls left and right, and on February 22, 1967, we went for a final check before departing the next day for icing tests.

"We again experienced a slight nibble going through 28,000 feet, but it went away. We continued climbing to what would be a more appro-

Before taking the first flight, the GII went through extensive "jump-off" tests. In this photo, the GII prototype is shown landing. *(Photo courtesy of Bob Smyth.)*

The GII is shown being readied for its maiden flight. Note the white border around the window. When the aircraft was being painted, the window was open, which prevented that small area from being painted. *(Photo courtesy of Bob Smyth.)*

priate cruise altitude for our trip west when at 36,000 feet, all hell broke loose. The airplane shook violently so that the instruments were a blur and two flight test engineers in the back could see the horizontal tail flapping up and down by looking aft through the windows. In no way is the tail normally visible through those windows; the tip had to be going up and down at least a foot."[34]

They immediately tried to reduce speed and altitude at the same time by cutting both engines back to idle, deploying the speed brakes and finally dropping the landing gear. After 50 seconds, the vibration stopped. "We landed without incident, inspected the tail, which was okay, and developed our oscillograph instrumentation, [used to measure vibration]," said Smyth.

The next day, they showed others at work the oscillograph recording, which showed the elevator trace diverging to a fairly large amplitude and then

remaining constant for 50 seconds. "When Gene Baird, our chief of Dynamics, saw it, he said, 'That's classical flutter,' like he had seen the Holy Grail," said Smyth. "We were fortunate we had a good strong Grumman airplane or we all would have been dead if the elevators had come off."[35]

The problem was traced to the balance weights on the leading edge of the elevator. There were three weights of equal length, two of stainless steel and one of tungsten, which is a heavier material. Apparently, the spanwise distribution of these weights was critical. The No. 1 airplane had it right, but the No. 2 airplane did not. The tails had been built by a subcontractor. Both airplanes were grounded for six weeks while they incorporated a paddle balance at the elevator tips, which added another 36 inch-pounds of balance to each elevator "for good measure," said Smyth. "The moral of the story for flight testers is to never get tunnel vision when you are chasing a problem; keep the larger picture in view and look for alternative causes."[36]

On October 19, 1967, the Gulfstream II was certified by the FAA and made its first public appearance that same month in Boston at the National Business Aviation Association's annual convention. Some people waited up to 45 minutes to get a look at the aircraft, which was in the static display area at Logan Airport.[37]

Aviation writers were enthusiastic. One article that appeared in *Aviation Week* proclaimed, "Grumman's reputation as a designer and supporter of quality aircraft — established in the business aviation field primarily by the Gulfstream I — has had an obvious impact on the Gulfstream II."[38]

The article stated that the Gulfstream II was a "solid, stable aircraft with an excess of power for any conceivable flight condition.... It combines direct user feedback with high performance and responsive handling qualities to produce a pilot's aircraft in all flight regimes."[39]

In the final analysis, the Gulfstream II was able to travel at Mach .85 fully loaded, with comfortable seating for 19 people in a cabin that was just a

Test pilot Bob Smyth receives a kiss from Sally Smyth, his wife, following the first flight of the GII on October 2, 1966. *(Photo courtesy of Bob Smyth.)*

foot longer than the original Gulfstream's. A modified interior could accommodate up to 30 passengers. The wing and T-tail were swept back 25 degrees. At that time, the GII would typically cruise at 39,000 feet and above, but the maximum ceiling was later raised to 45,000 feet. It also had a trans-Atlantic cruising capability of Mach .75. The GII could take off from an airfield 4,300 feet long and land on a 3,500-foot runway.

Attracting buyers was not a problem, even with its $2 million price tag. More than 40 had been ordered even before the aircraft was certified, shooting down the conventional wisdom that aircraft over $1 million would never sell.[40] On January 6, 1968, the first customer's Gulfstream II, s/n 005, was outfitted and handed over to National Distillers & Chemical Corporation, a customer of the Gulfstream I.[41]

By the time the GII took flight, the visionary who foresaw aircraft designed for the pursuit of business, Leroy Grumman, had stepped down. Seventy-one years old and suffering from virtual blindness, Grumman retired from active participation in 1966 to be replaced by Leon "Jake" Swirbul as president until his death, at which time Clint Towl took over as chairman of the board. Lew Evans became president, and Bill Schwendler was chairman of the executive steering committee. By that time, Grumman Aerospace, as it was then called, employed more than 33,000 workers.

Henry Schiebel (left) hands over the keys to National Distillers pilot Harold Curtis. Schiebel was one of the fathers of the Gulfstream program. *(Photo courtesy of Gulfstream Aerospace.)*

Gulfstream Moves to Savannah, Georgia

As the Gulfstream II program was getting underway, Grumman officials wanted to separate civil and military aircraft lines to improve efficiency and thereby cut costs.[42] They decided they could best accomplish this by moving the civilian Gulfstream program to a separate building in Bethpage or even another location entirely.[43]

After an extensive search, Grumman officials decided on Savannah in 1966. In a statement about the move, Lew Evans said that of the many sites looked at, Savannah, Georgia, most closely met the basic criteria for development of a consolidated commercial aircraft facility because of "a potential supply of skilled labor, an established airfield adjacent to the plant site, sufficient acreage for future plant expansion, availability of adequate transportation facilities suitable for heavy equip-

ment and machinery, and weather conditions favorable to year-round flight testing and flight training operations."[44]

The city of Savannah added another incentive as well by approving $7.5 million in Special Purpose Airport Revenue Bonds to finance the construction of a 260,000-square-foot building, which would be leased by Grumman. The facility, located on a 110-acre site adjacent to Travis Field, would house production and flight testing for the GII. Once the bonds were approved by the city and the Savannah Airport Commission, construction of Grumman's new facility started in late 1966.[45]

Although a spot had been secured, there was still one other major problem: No one wanted to go there. "It was a very good selection," recalled Albert

"Goldie" Glenn, service manager at the time and later president of the company. "The only trouble was that all the people who had all the experience didn't want to go to Savannah. Nobody wanted to go to Savannah. Including me."[46]

Grumman was a very close-knit community, and its people felt loyalty to and a sense of investment in the company. Moving a company program away from its Bethpage birthplace was outside what many felt was the Grumman tradition. It was an uncomfortable move.[47]

Still, Grumman forged ahead. In June 1967, the company opened the new facility at Travis Field. The plant hired 90 percent of the 100 employees from the Savannah community. In a ceremony announcing the opening, Grumman President Lew Evans said, "I have been very much impressed with city and state officials who have done their very best to provide the kind of environment in which the Grumman company can successfully produce its aeronautical products. I believe the results will be mutually beneficial to both Grumman and the citizens of Savannah." The first GII to be completed in Savannah, s/n 008, flew on November 15, 1967.[48]

There were problems with the move to Savannah that would take years to iron out. Not only did Grummanites balk at moving to Savannah, but the service centers in both locations competed with one another for service work. Those left in Bethpage didn't want to give up their end of the Gulfstream program, and they didn't want to leave "the head shed," explained Glenn. "Mr. Schwendler had been such a great supporter of the program. Everyone feared we wouldn't get the support we had because we would go back to priority given to military programs."[49]

Glenn too had held onto his desk with white knuckles, but in 1969 he was sent to Savannah anyway. When he tried to get back to Bethpage, he was bluntly told by the president, "That is your job. You have no job back at Bethpage." Glenn said every day was a battle for the right tools, the right parts and the right people. Furthermore, Bethpage was located closer to most of Gulfstream's customers, a situation exploited by the Bethpage service staff. "They called customers directly to get the business to keep their service center going," Glenn explained. "They told customers that they knew all about the airplanes, and that the guys in Savannah were too new and inexperienced."

Savannah gradually accumulated the tools, the staffing and the experience needed to win service work. Employment gradually rose from 100 workers to more than 1,700 people working on various subassemblies for the GI and GII. As production and service work transferred to Savannah, space in Bethpage was freed up to allow Grumman to concentrate on filling military contracts.

Finally, Glenn wrote a memo to Grumman management stating that the Bethpage service plant was going to be closed and all service work was to be centered in Savannah.

This wasn't the end of Glenn's struggle with the home office, however. The chain of command still led back to Bethpage, and it was a chain his

Right: Grumman President Lew Evans (left) is welcomed to Savannah, Georgia. *(Photo courtesy of Albert Glenn.)*

Below: An aerial view of the Savannah site. Moving Gulfstream to Savannah was not popular. No one wanted to give up the program, but no one wanted to move to Georgia. *(Photo courtesy of the Grumman History Center.)*

Above: The Savannah workforce took time to train, but many have spent their careers working there. Pictured from left to right are Ann Stille, Billie Lewis and Knoxie Crocker. Crocker went on to become Savannah's first female foreperson, appointed by Goldie Glenn. *(Photo courtesy of the Grumman History Center.)*

Right: The chariot of the kings, a GII in flight. The GII found ready acceptance among business leaders and heads of state. *(Photo courtesy of the Grumman History Center.)*

superiors liked to jerk from time to time. (See Chapter Four.)[50]

Fit for a King

Meanwhile, the GII program was an unqualified success. Operators of the GI readily embraced its successor, with Campbell Soup; Procter & Gamble; Ford; Texaco; Time, Inc. and United States Steel among the GII's customers. Even aerospace giant Northrop Corporation was a customer. Northrop was the first to receive a certificate to operate the GII as a charter aircraft. This particular GII, N8000J, was chartered for the film *The Disappearance of Flight 412* in 1972.[51] The U.S. Coast Guard became a customer as well when it purchased one to be used as a VIP and staff trans-

port. The Rockefeller family, American "royalty," also bought a GII.

Outfitting the interiors of the aircraft proved every bit as unusual and difficult as Bill Schwendler and Leroy Grumman predicted it would. From the very start of the Gulfstream program, they insisted that the distributor be the one to install the interiors and most of the avionics to the customer's specifications. Although this was an area that was very profitable, management believed that Grumman's job was to build the aircraft. One owner requested storage space for 16 magnums of champagne. Another customer had a Yamaha electric organ installed, allowing him to play while airborne.[52] In most cases, the customer and outfitting agency would come back

to Grumman for approval in order to maintain structural integrity.

Toward the end of the sixties, the GII was breaking records regularly. On May 4, 1968, for instance, N100P became the first corporate aircraft to fly nonstop from the United States to Europe. Taking off from Teterboro, New Jersey, the aircraft landed at Gatwick, England, after six hours and 55 minutes of flight. It wasn't long before such flights, with a friendly tailwind, became commonplace.

The GII's range, comfort and prestige were such that royalty around the world became customers. This was especially true in the Middle East, where members of royal families wanted the ability to fly nonstop from point to point in the interest of security. Joseph Anckner, the group leader in charge of the GII mock-up, became an international salesman, with most of his early sales going to Arab nations in the Middle East. "A lot of Arab leaders did not want to stop until they reached their destination," he noted.[53]

But as the GII broke records, the national economy was heading into a tailspin. Inflation, interest rates and unemployment were all on the rise, leading economic pundits to describe the malaise as "stagflation." Workers had toiled long and hard to bring the Savannah plant up to speed, but the plant would soon be threatened with closure.

Grumman American Aviation Corporation: the report on 1973, our first year.

The merger of the Gulfstream program and American Aviation was the first step toward independence.
(Photo courtesy of Joseph Anckner.)

CHAPTER FOUR

THE WINDS OF CHANGE

1970–1977

*"Every day somebody else was coming down here telling me how
things were going to run.... I'm just sitting here struggling with everyone
telling me they're my boss."*

— Albert "Goldie" Glenn, after the
Gulfstream program was merged
with American Aviation[1]

GRUMMAN AEROSPACE WAS
caught in a merciless vise.
Once-profitable military programs were bleeding money because
inflation was running rampant, costs
were spiraling out of control, and the
federal government refused to renegotiate contracts that had been settled when
interest rates hovered at a balmy 3 percent.

By 1971, the inflation situation had grown so
dire that President Richard Nixon froze wages and
prices for 90 days. Nixon's decision was a complete about-face because he had long insisted
that he would never resort to such drastic measures. In fact, wage and price controls had no
practical effect on holding down interest rates or
increasing employment.[2] In the general aviation
industry, production reverted to what it had been
back in 1960.

The effect of stagflation on the new Savannah
facility was catastrophic. Just three years after
opening the facility, Grumman slashed the
Savannah workforce from 1,700 to about 700.
Plant Manager Fred Eckert told the local media
that the layoffs were the result of the current economic conditions, which in turn caused a reduction in production of the Gulfstream II aircraft.[3]
To keep even this reduced workforce busy,
Savannah began building passenger railcars to be
used as the Seattle/Tacoma Airport shuttles.
About 12 cars were built under the contract

before conditions improved enough
to return to aircraft production.

The Savannah cutbacks coincided
with a layoff of about 1,200 engineers
at Grumman's Bethpage facility. As
the recession continued, Grumman
laid off a total of about 10,000 workers
from its 33,000 workforce.

The year 1971 ended with Grumman's first
loss since it opened for business in 1930. With
sales dropping by almost 20 percent, no dividends
were paid to shareholders for the first time since
going public.[4] The next year was even worse, ending with a loss of $70 million on sales of nearly
$700 million.[5] The Savannah facility made its small
payroll during this difficult time in large part by the
work coming into the service center. There was talk
in Bethpage about shutting down the Savannah
plant altogether.[6]

Then tragedy struck in 1972 when Lew Evans,
president and CEO of Grumman Aerospace, suffered a heart attack and died. John C. Bierwirth,
a former executive with National Distillers &
Chemical Corporation, was selected to lead the
organization because of his financial acumen.

This is a logo from the brochure marketing the T-cat, part of
the light aircraft line of American Aviation, which merged with
Grumman's Gulfstream program.

For the first time, an engineer would not lead Grumman as president.[7]

The Genesis of Grumman American Aviation

Several days after Bierwirth took control, he was handed a folder that had belonged to Evans. The folder contained a report on a light aircraft company called American Aviation Corporation, based in Cleveland, that Evans had been interested in purchasing in 1969. Evans, in much the same spirit as Leroy Grumman, wanted to build products for the civilian market so that the company didn't have to rely on its main customer, the ever-fickle U.S. military, to stay solvent.

Evans had contacted Russell Meyer, who was president and CEO of American Aviation, and the two men explored the possibility of a merger. American Aviation had just started production of the American Yankee, a spunky two-seat airplane, and came out with a modified version called the

Above: These dramatic photos show the last seconds of flight of the F-14 Tomcat as a hydraulic failure forced pilots Bob Smyth and Bill Miller to bail out. Smyth is in the higher of the two parachutes. Miller ejected as the fighter pitched toward the ground. *(Photos courtesy of Bob Smyth.)*

Left: *Flying* magazine featuring the Yankee, a sporty two-seat derivative of the Bede BD-1. *(Photo courtesy of Albert Glenn.)*

November 1967/75¢

FLYING

World's most widely read aviation magazine

Exclusive:
First Flight
in the
YANKEE
(Son of Bede)

Think Twice
About
SPECIAL VFR

Pilot Reports:
Beech
King Air

The FH-1100

Trainer. American Aviation got its start in the early 1960s producing a version of the homebuilt Bede BD-1 aircraft, a two-seat light plane known for its revolutionary construction method. Rather than being riveted, the aircraft was bonded together to form a smooth finish.[8] The design later grew into a family of two- and four-seat light aircraft. By 1972, American Aviation had produced 450 single-engine aircraft in its small Cleveland plant but was still losing money.[9]

Negotiations between Evans and Meyer had been set on the back burner. Evans had to contend with other problems, namely the F-14

Tomcat program and the fact that it was hemorrhaging money. The program was a fixed-cost contract with the U.S. Navy, and stagflation quickly shoved Grumman into the red.

The Tomcat was destined to become the Navy's standard carrier-based fighter. With its variable-geometry wings, which can automatically swing to and from a delta configuration to increase speed or maneuverability, the Tomcat made every other fighter of its time obsolete.

But during its second flight, which was made before a gathering of Navy brass, the Tomcat's hydraulic system failed while the aircraft was less than 1,000 feet from the ground. The test pilots, Bob Smyth and Bill Miller, ejected from the falling aircraft just before it hit the ground; they landed safely a few yards away from the burning wreckage and just a half mile short of the runway.

Grumman Aerospace appeared to be heading toward a similar ending because the cost overruns were strangling the company. The Navy refused to renegotiate the fixed-cost contracts. Some executives within Grumman worried about the company's solvency and the effect the military prob-

lems could have on its premier civilian program — the Gulfstream.

As Grumman struggled against the tide of red ink — losing $220 million on the original Tomcat contract — Bierwirth decided to go ahead with the merger.[10] In early August 1972, Grumman Aerospace agreed to merge its Gulfstream program, including the GI and GII, with American Aviation, forming Grumman American Aviation.

Initially, Grumman Aerospace owned 80 percent of the new venture, with the owners of American Aviation retaining 20 percent. The new board of directors was a combination of executives and directors from Grumman and American Aviation. Bierwirth, Clint Towl (then chairman of Grumman Aerospace) and Senior Vice President John Carr came from Grumman. From American Aviation came Russ Meyer, who stayed on as president and CEO; Art Modell, then owner of the Cleveland Browns (and, as of 2000, owner of the Baltimore Ravens); David S. Ingalls, Jr., son of a famous businessman and aviator (his father had become America's first ace during World War I); and Duane Stranahan, who hails from the family that established Champion Spark Plugs.

The subsidiary was one of several Grumman set up during this time for different operations within the company. The corporate headquarters remained in Cleveland.[11] "The move amounts to a minor diversification by Grumman," noted *Aviation International News*, "but is a major step for the Cleveland-based American Aviation, which made a profit last year on total sales of $4 million."[12] There was another advantage for Grumman besides protecting its crown jewel, the Gulfstream program. Merging Gulfstream and American Aviation gave Grumman a $4.3 million tax benefit going forward in 1973.

It was not to be a happy marriage. The minority shareholders who had the most stock — Modell, Stranahan and Ingalls — were all strong-willed and successful men. When they struck the deal with Bierwirth, all three preferred stock rather than cash. After the marriage broke up in 1978, *Forbes* published a postmortem:

"The old owners of American Aviation weren't interested in cash.... For combining their $4.8 million in assets with Grumman's $28 million

Russ Meyer became president of Grumman's new subsidiary, Grumman American Aviation. Meyer found himself in the middle of a tug-of-war between Grumman Aerospace and Grumman American's board of directors. *(Photo courtesy of Cessna.)*

they ended up with 20 percent of the new subsidiary's stock plus warrants to buy another 23 percent in 1977 or 1978. Why would Grumman give up so much? The tax-loss carry forward, says Bierwirth: 'It created a $4.3 million Grumman tax benefit.'"[13]

Modell, Stranahan and Ingalls exercised their right as soon as they could. By 1977, they owned 43 percent of the stock of Grumman American, or almost half the company. And they were not hands-off managers. The *Forbes* article noted that the tax write-off "was an expensive benefit. It set in motion a chain of events that would make it impossible for Grumman to keep the Gulfstream."[14]

But in the beginning, Grumman American was an exciting place to work. "I couldn't wait to get up in the morning," commented Russ Meyer in a 1999 interview. "We thought Grumman American was the best company in the world and we were, by God, committed."[15] The Savannah operation was gaining momentum as employees were hired back. Eventually, the service center in Bethpage was closed because the Savannah center had the training and the tools to do the job. In conjunction with the closing in Bethpage, the Savannah Service Center expanded by 32,000 square feet for GII fleet support, and a product support department was set up and run by Goldie Glenn. A new 8,000-square-foot FlightSafety training center was added with state-of-the-art GII simulators. It was FlightSafety's very first remote facility, recalled Russ Meyer. Al Ueltschi, the man who founded the pioneering flight training company, supplied the simulator and the training, and Grumman American gave type ratings to the crew. Recurrent training was conducted in Savannah as well.[16]

Savannah was becoming a one-stop shop for the Gulfstream aircraft. "We brought everything together.... We were building the airplane, we were servicing it, and we were doing all the training here," recalled Albert Glenn. Glenn's business cards at the time had the words "service manager" printed on them, but the title was a misnomer. His role and responsibilities exceeded his title; he was critical in getting Savannah running as a first-class service center. Charles Coppi, meanwhile, was transferred to Savannah to begin expanding and building the technical operations.

Too Many Cooks

Weaning the Savannah facility from dependence on Bethpage remained a struggle. Gulfstream salesmen, for instance, were still centered in Grumman's main plant. They, like many others, held on to their Bethpage desks with white knuckles because they didn't want to transfer to Savannah. On several occasions, Russ Meyer forced the issue of consolidating all of the necessary authority and resources in Savannah. But with the chain of command still leading back to Bethpage, even scheduling service was difficult. Glenn had to borrow workers from the production line to fill in at the service end. "I had to go beg to get people to work on a customer's airplane," Glenn recalled. "They'd go from the production side to the service side for a while and then go back to production. Customers would come in and raise hell with me because no one was working on their airplanes."[17]

Glenn managed to complete the transition of service to Savannah, but factions in Bethpage continued to contend for control of Grumman American. "Every day somebody else was coming down here telling me how things were going to run," Glenn said. "In the meantime, I'm just sitting here struggling with everyone telling me they're my boss, but Russ Meyer was the president and CEO."[18]

In spite of the interference from the home office, Meyer was able to launch several initiatives in 1972 and 1973 that helped sales and increased revenue. Grumman American began an emphasis on marketing and direct selling, for instance, instead of working through distributors. In addition, Grumman American offered an aircraft called the AgCat, used specifically for crop dusting. Employees from the light plane operation in Cleveland, Ohio, were relocated to Savannah to develop and produce a line of light aircraft that included the two-seat T-cat and Trainer, as well as the four-place Cheetah, Cougar and Traveler.[19]

Grumman American's performance was impressive given the seemingly endless crises that confronted the United States in the early and mid-seventies. The Arab oil boycott, for instance, had led to the chilling prospect of fuel allocation for general aviation. Oil stocks, in fact, were relatively full nationwide, but the panic created the perception that there was a fuel shortage. The reaction did in fact cause a shortage where one did not previously exist.

Russell Meyer, then chairman of the General Aviation Manufacturers Association, worked with others in the aviation industry to ensure that the industry received its fair share of fuel. A year later, in 1974, the fuel situation had brightened considerably, but then U.S. businesses again faced a worsening economy. The effect on Grumman American was slight, with sales falling from $86 million to $82.7 million between 1973 and 1974.

The Shuttle Program

Amid the political and economic uncertainties during this period came a singular and unique honor: In 1973, NASA selected the Gulfstream II as the new Shuttle Training Aircraft (STA), which would be used to train shuttle astronauts.

NASA ordered two GIIs for the mission. The space agency selected the GII because its fuel load was large enough to allow for prolonged training sessions and it could achieve an altitude of more than 43,000 feet. This was important because it allowed an astronaut more time to learn how to adjust a gliding aircraft coming in for an approach. Furthermore, the GII's airframe was rugged enough to permit design changes if the design of the shuttle was modified.[20]

The contract, while a coup for Grumman American, was bittersweet for Grumman Aerospace. The parent company had lost the bid to develop the world's first reusable spacecraft to Rockwell International. (Grumman was subcontracted to build the shuttle's wings, however.)

The program had been conceived in the 1960s as a more cost-effective way to deliver new satellites and repair older satellites, as well as to conduct scientific experiments without a permanent space station.

The Gulfstreams, designated N946NA and N947NA, were built to a standard GII configuration in Savannah and then sent to Bethpage, where engineers modified the aircraft to simulate the approach and landing characteristics of the space shuttle. This was a challenge because the GII had a basic weight of 62,200 pounds. By contrast, the shuttle weighed in at 250,000 pounds and was capable of flying only as a hypersonic glider within the atmosphere.

To simulate the characteristics of the shuttle during its landing sequence, special in-flight thrust reversers were added to duplicate drag. Direct-lift flaps were installed, which subjected the cockpit to the same G forces as would be experienced in the shuttle. Two side force generators, controlled by a computer, protruded from under the wings like two large rudders to simulate the shuttle's predicted sideward movement.

Inside the aircraft, the left side of the cockpit was designed to resemble the shuttle cockpit; on

In 1973, Grumman American won a contract from NASA to convert two GIIs into Shuttle Training Aircraft. Note the vertical sideforce generators extending from the bottom of the aircraft. These helped to replicate the performance characteristics of the space shuttle as it glided through the atmosphere. *(Photo courtesy of George Viteritti.)*

the right side, an instructor sat before a standard GII instrument panel to which a computer had been added. The instructor punched in variables to simulate the shuttle's weight, center of gravity reference, barometric setting and desired landing coordinates. During training, the aircraft would climb to 35,000 feet, then plunge to 50 feet in less than three minutes to mirror the shuttle's extreme rate of descent.[21]

The Shuttle Training Aircraft were delivered to the Lyndon B. Johnson Space Center in Houston, Texas, in 1975. Each aircraft was scheduled to fly about 30 hours per month. The majority of the flights took place at the Northrup Strip, a dry-lake runway at the southwestern edge of the White Sands Missile Range in southern New Mexico.[22] On April 12, 1981, the shuttle Columbia flew into space for the first time, piloted by astronauts who trained for their historic flight in a Gulfstream II.

Ground Battles

Meanwhile, as these two GIIs were being built, the situation in Grumman American's board was rocketing out of control. With so many managerial hands in one pie, it was perhaps inevitable that meetings grew more contentious. In the middle was Russ Meyer, Grumman American's chief executive officer. "Meyer had been a CEO," noted a *Forbes* article years later. "Now he felt like a division manager, compelled to clear everything with Grumman's Bethpage headquarters."[23]

Meyer had received an offer from Cessna in 1973, which he turned down. "I told Dwane Wallace [chairman of Cessna], 'I just can't leave. I built the company. I've hired most of the employees. We're doing well and I like what I'm doing."[24] Wallace, who had helped his uncle, Cessna founder Clyde Cessna, rebuild the aircraft company, was undeterred. He returned six months later with a broader offer. The challenge and opportunities Cessna presented at that time were too great to walk away from. In the summer of 1974 Meyer decided to leave to become an executive vice president with the Cessna Aircraft Company. He soon led the organization as president, CEO and chairman.

Bierwirth installed longtime Grummanite Corwin "Corky" Meyer — no relation to Russ

The shuttle Columbia being piggybacked after its historic flight as the world's first reusable spacecraft.
(Photo courtesy of Federal-Mogul.)

Above: The Cheetah was a redesigned version of the popular four-seat Traveler. *(Photo courtesy of Albert Glenn.)*

Below: Corwin "Corky" Meyer (right) with Grumman employee Earl Schaeffer. Meyer replaced Russ Meyer (no relation), who left Grumman American to lead Cessna. *(Photo courtesy of Earl Schaeffer.)*

Meyer — to lead Grumman American, a move which infuriated the minority shareholders. Ingalls, Modell and Stranahan wanted a greater say in managing Grumman American.[25]

In the meantime, Grumman American was prospering. Goldie Glenn's title finally caught up with his responsibilities when he became vice president and general manager of the Savannah operation in 1974. By May 1975, Meyer announced that light airplane production in Savannah would double in the next five years, jumping from about 500 aircraft per year to 1,000. More space was needed to accommodate the expansion, so another 180,000 square feet in new buildings was either under construction or planned that year, including a large warehouse next to the main plant at Travis Field, a bonding shop, a final assembly shop and a painting facility.

Hundreds of light aircraft including the Cheetah, Trainer, T-cat, Tiger and twin-engine Cougar were eventually produced in Savannah. The Cheetah was a redesigned version of the popular four-seat Traveler, which was built in Cleveland

until 1975.[26] It featured, among other things, a redesigned engine cowling and tail surfaces.[27] "We gained in speed, styling and simplicity by redesigning the cooling baffles, engine cowling, exhaust system and landing gear fairings," Corky Meyer told *Plane & Pilot* in December 1975. "In addition, our engineers who helped design the Gulfstream II corporate jet did some remarkable improvements to both the instrument panel and general pilot and passenger comfort areas."[28] The Tiger, which was introduced in 1975, was another four-seat aircraft.[29]

During a time of fuel conservation, Grumman American advertised its light airplanes, such as the T-cat and Lynx pictured below, as fuel-efficient transportation alternatives. *(Photo courtesy of Albert Glenn.)*

The Grumman American Trainer was a two-seat aircraft designed and engineered for flight training and instruction. It featured, among other things, a bubble canopy for increased visibility.[30] The two-seat T-cat was also a trainer produced by Grumman American and was priced under $20,000.[31]

The only light aircraft completely developed and produced in Savannah was the GA-7 and its deluxe version, known as the Cougar. The GA-7 twin had an enclosed cabin of aluminum honeycomb construction and, as with the Grumman American singles, made use of metal-to-metal bonding throughout its airframe.[32] The production prototype was first flown on January 12, 1977, and it was certified in September of that year. Deliveries from Savannah began in early 1978.[33]

The Cougar met with only limited success. In the post–energy crisis period, the demand for four-seat

The Grumman American T-cat and Lynx.

You tell us, which one is the trainer?

Actually, they both are or can be. Or either one can be a sporty two placer to rent or to own. To give you the performance you want, we designed out all the things you don't need, like doors to adjust, oleo struts to leak, and rivets all over the place to slow you down. Quite simply, nobody

gives you the speed, the miles per gallon, and the easy to fly and fix simplicity that Grumman American does. Nobody. (Just look at the figures: The Lynx can deliver a 134 mph cruise speed from a 115 hp engine using 100 octane low lead fuel.) And, when you step into a T-cat or Lynx,

you're joining the Grumman American Eagle Squadron, fighting for energy efficiency to save your country's fuel. The Grumman American T-cat and the deluxe Lynx. Everything you'd expect and a whole lot more.

twin-engined aircraft was minimal. Only 115 GA-7s and Cougars were built by Grumman American.[34]

By the end of 1976, Grumman American and its Savannah headquarters were continuing on an upward swing, and the Savannah facility had increased in size by 60 percent to approximately 540,000 square feet. Sales of the GII exceeded expectations, topping out at 21, which was the highest number sold by the company in one year since the late 1960s.[35]

The GII was nearing the end of its development cycle. A tip-tank version had been introduced to satisfy the immediate need for more range, but it was time for Grumman American to take the next step in the evolution of the Gulfstream program.

The Gulfstream III — The First Design

Unfortunately, the next step was a step too far in terms of both price and research and development costs. It was clearly too much airplane for the market and too much of a financial burden for the company. Cost and price aside, the original design for the Gulfstream III compromised on nothing.

By the middle of the seventies, international business flying was on the rise as corporations started tapping into overseas markets. Along with this, executives had an increasing need to get to international destinations as quickly and efficiently as possible.

The Gulfstream II aircraft had been designed primarily for coast-to-coast nonstop flights within the United States, and operators had routinely used the GII to cross the Atlantic and Pacific oceans. However, the aircraft's range generally did not permit nonstop flights to most international destinations, particularly against strong headwinds.

The program, officially known as the Gulfstream X program because it was very low-key, was announced in November 1976. The design built upon the success of the GII. Slightly larger and heavier, the aircraft was to achieve greater range, speed and fuel capacity.

In order to guarantee making a nonstop international flight against the worst possible headwinds, the aircraft's range had to be at least 4,000 nautical miles, about 1,200 nautical miles greater than the range of the Gulfstream II. To accomplish the flight in a little more than eight hours — a rea-

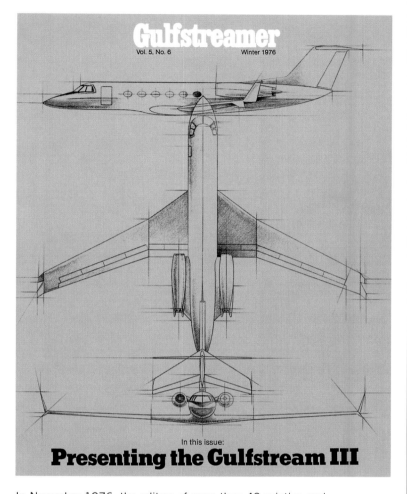

Gulfstreamer
Vol. 5, No. 6   Winter 1976

In this issue:
Presenting the Gulfstream III

In November 1976, the editors of more than 40 aviation and business publications gathered at the Wings Club in New York for Gulfstream American's formal announcement of the GIII. The GIII's original design proved to be a step too far, however. *(Photo courtesy of Gulfstream Aerospace.)*

sonable amount of time which would prevent crew fatigue — the aircraft would have to cruise at speeds higher than Mach .8.[36] The cockpit was made large enough to accommodate three people, and the fuselage was stretched four feet. As a result, the proposed aircraft would have weighed 73,700 pounds in gross weight, which meant an entirely new landing gear had to be developed.

And, for the first time, market surveys included such concerns as fuel conservation and pollution controls among the items on the wish list. On the one hand, potential customers wanted more range, faster speed, increased comfort and greater seating capacity; on the other, the aircraft had to demonstrate better fuel efficiency than in the past and adhere to new environmental regulations governing emissions and noise.

Balancing the two was a thorny engineering challenge, especially in the area of emission and noise reduction, because regulations were evolving and didn't always reflect what could actually be accomplished by engineers. "Aircraft noise and engine emissions posed both a problem and a dilemma," noted the AIAA GIII case study, written by engineers Charles Coppi, Lawrence Mead and John Strakosch.

"The Gulfstream X project was launched in the midst of a cloudy debate amongst the EPA, the FAA and the industry as to the actual detrimental impact of noise, engine smoke and engine gaseous emissions on the air quality and the public health and welfare. Further, the proposed requirements, standards and compliance dates were marginally definitive."[37]

A modified Rolls-Royce Spey engine, the GII's power plant, was again selected because it best suited the power, fuel consumption, noise level (noise dampening kits had recently been introduced for the engine) and emission requirements.

Perhaps the most dramatic improvement was the design of a new wing that took advantage of the latest supercritical aerodynamic technology. The redesigned wing was part of the trade-off between range/speed requirements and the emerging environmental and fuel regulations. The 800-square-foot wing reduced drag. The wing could also be retrofitted to GII aircraft.

The wings were designed with winglets — vertical airfoils attached to the wingtips. The winglet was an innovation that came from NASA's research into more fuel-efficient designs. The program itself was the response to the Middle East oil embargo in 1973, a rude awakening for Americans long accustomed to relatively cheap and plentiful oil supplies.[38]

When it was unveiled in late 1976, the GIII's specifications were jaw-droppers: On paper, the airplane had a range of 4,400 nautical miles and cruised at Mach .84. *Aviation Week & Space Technology* noted that "No business jet flying today, with the exception of converted airliners, comes close to meeting this combination of numbers.

"Through the use of a unique and futuristic looking design ... composed of a modified supercritical airfoil with winglets at

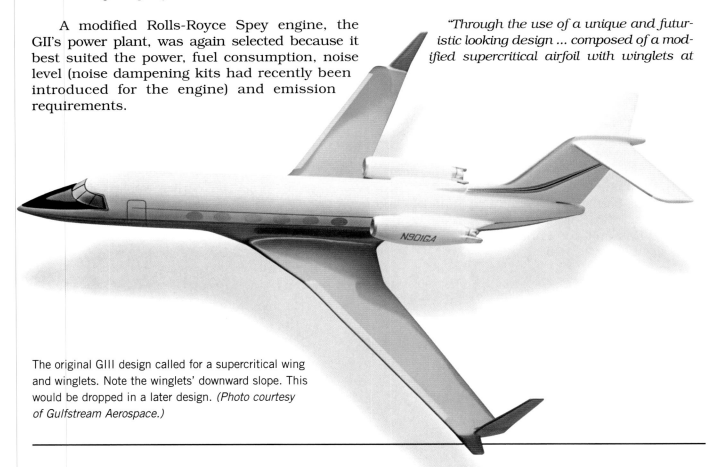

The original GIII design called for a supercritical wing and winglets. Note the winglets' downward slope. This would be dropped in a later design. *(Photo courtesy of Gulfstream Aerospace.)*

each tip, Grumman American claims its Gulfstream III will be able to obtain 35 percent more range and 17 percent more speed for the same amount of cruise thrust as in the Gulfstream II."[39]

Striking a Balance

But the GIII as originally envisioned was scrapped in June 1977 because the research and development costs were spiraling out of control. The feasibility of the design was never in question, according to aviation writers Steve Saunders and Ian Woodhouse. "Indeed, the design was virtually a technical reality."[40] Wind tunnel tests had been conducted and a master program schedule had been established. Furthermore, 40 orders had been secured.

"[Grumman American] calculated that the cost to develop the Gulfstream III expressed in terms of 1980 to 1983 dollars would make the aircraft's development infeasible.... Even if the go-ahead was to be given, the resulting high price for each aircraft would be a deterrent to its success in a very competitive market."[41]

The aircraft was originally supposed to cost somewhere in the $7 million range, but Grumman American would have to price it at more than $12 million.

There was another phenomenon taking place throughout business aviation around the time the GIII program was put on hold: American business aircraft manufacturers faced formidable competition. "Never before had such an impressive array of new models been offered," remarked Saunders and Woodhouse. "Rockwell, Cessna, Gates Learjet, France's Dassault and Canada's Canadair were all rushing to beat each other with their developments, and, in addition, Beech Aircraft Corporation and Japan's Mitsubishi Heavy Industries were considering whether to launch their first executive jets."[42]

Design 38D, the designation of the GIII program, needed to be revamped in order to keep research and development costs in check while still remaining true to the performance characteristics operators wanted.

Faced with these challenges, Grumman officials did what they had done in the past and turned to Gulfstream customers for their opinion. Specifically, Grumman wanted to know if a relaxation in the performance standards would be acceptable. A revised survey was conducted, and Design 38D was replaced by Design 38E, which included the following criteria:[43]

- 3,600 minimum nautical mile range
- .78 to .8 Mach cruise speed
- Fuel efficiency 15 to 20 percent better than the Gulfstream II
- Airport performance equal to or better than Gulfstream II

With the new characteristics in mind, Coppi and his engineers went to work scaling down the original Gulfstream III. By the spring of 1978, the newest GIII prototype was taking shape. It included a larger fuselage, a more pointed nose and a highly modified semi-supercritical wing with NASA-type winglets. It was based more closely on its predecessor, the Gulfstream II. The reconfigured GIII retained 90 percent of the original design requirements for 30 percent of the development cost.

"Gone was the new wing design, as the new Gulfstream III was to use the wings of the existing aircraft with the addition of winglets. The not-so-drastic recontouring of the forward fuselage as proposed earlier was retained, but the increase in fuselage length was limited to a more modest 2 feet," wrote aviation author Rene Francillon.[44]

But by the time the Gulfstream III flew from the drawing board to the skies, more than just the Gulfstream program had changed. The break from Grumman American would be complete, and the Gulfstream program would transform into a corporation unto itself.

1978
Allen Paulson buys Grumman American and changes the name to Gulfstream American.

1979
The GIII's first flight takes place on December 2.

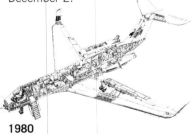

1980
The FAA certifies the GIII in September.

1981
Gulfstream American acquires Rockwell Aviation Division in Bethany, Oklahoma.

1982
Name changed to Gulfstream Aerospace Corporation.

1982
Go-ahead given to develop the GIV.

1983
The company goes public and shares sell out by the end of the day.

1984
Gulfstream becomes a *Fortune* 500 company.

1985
Chrysler buys Gulfstream.

1985
The GIV flies for the first time on September 19.

1986

Gulfstream purchases AiResearch Aviation Completion Center in Long Beach, California.

1986

Allen Paulson receives the Wright Brothers Memorial Trophy for his contributions to aviation.

1990

Chrysler announces that Gulfstream is up for sale. The company is purchased by Forstmann Little & Company, with Paulson as chairman and CEO.

Allen Paulson was catapulted into prominence when he bought Grumman American. *(Photo courtesy of Gulfstream Aerospace.)*

CHAPTER FIVE

OUT OF LEFT FIELD

1978–1979

"When Jimmy Carter was running for president, the wags where saying, 'Jimmy who?' Recently, at the announcement of the sale of Grumman American Aviation Corp. to American Jet Industries, the question 'AJI and Allen Who?' was making the rounds."

— *Aviation International News*, 1978[1]

THE HOWLING BLIZZARD WAS called simply "Storm No. 9," but it took almost a thousand snowplows to keep the principal roads in New York City's five boroughs even marginally open. The blizzard lashed New York for two days in early February of 1978, costing the city $8.5 million to clean up.[2]

Inside the Waldorf-Astoria, where the board members of Grumman American Aviation were meeting to resolve their differences, raged a different sort of storm. There was a lot to argue about. The Gulfstream III project continued to rankle the three main minority shareholders, known collectively as the Cleveland Group: David Ingalls, Art Modell and Duane Stranahan. Before the original GIII design was scrapped, Grumman American had invested more than $120 million in its research and development, double what was expected, and that did not include the prototype. For several years, the Cleveland Group had insisted on hiring outside bidders or consultants to finish the design. They felt that Grumman American's president and chief executive officer, longtime Grummanite Corwin "Corky" Meyer, was more concerned with the interests of Grumman Aerospace than he was with the interests of Grumman American's shareholders.[3]

The minority shareholders were also upset over an investigation launched by the Securities and Exchange Commission into alleged foreign payments involving the sale of F-14 fighters and Gulfstreams. The investigation had cast a cloud over Grumman American because its leading sales distributor, Page Airways, was accused of paying off foreign government officials in Africa and elsewhere to encourage the purchase of the Gulfstream II. Ultimately, the investigation would result in $120,000 in fines for Grumman American.[4]

The SEC investigation prevented Modell, Ingalls and Stranahan from exercising their warrants to buy another 23 percent of Grumman American stock, which would consolidate 43 percent of the company in their hands, with Grumman Aerospace holding the balance.[5]

Bierwirth was angry as well. The line of light aircraft that came with the American Aviation reverse merger (the Trainer, Traveler, Tiger, Cheetah, Cougar and so on) wasn't turning a profit. He was fed up with clashing constantly with the three shareholders and refused to bring in outsiders to manage the engineering for the Gulfstream program.

At the Waldorf-Astoria, the minority shareholders issued an ultimatum: either buy them out at $8.50 a share, or remove Corky Meyer and allow

---

Allen Paulson quickly changed the name of Grumman American to Gulfstream American to reflect the company's flagship product.

Boardroom infighting would soon lead to the sale of the Savannah-based Grumman American even though sales of the GII were breaking records. *(Photo courtesy of Gulfstream Aerospace.)*

Grumman American to operate with more autonomy — which meant more outside directors and its own audit committee. They threatened to sue if Bierwirth didn't agree.[6]

Rising Sales

The disputes belied the fact that Grumman American — SEC investigation and mounting R&D costs notwithstanding — was building and selling more Gulfstreams than it had in years. Deliveries of the GII had passed the 200 mark, and orders from areas outside the United States, including Europe and the Middle East, increased significantly during this time. There was also rising interest in the Gulfstream from South America, particularly oil-rich Venezuela, and continuing interest in Africa, where six Gulfstream IIs operated in six different countries.[7]

Grumman American employees got to share in this success when, in November 1977, President Corky Meyer announced an across-the-board pay increase for all employees of $15.20 a week or $793 a year. "We will continue keeping Grumman American one of the best places to work in the country," Meyer told the employees in a 15-minute address.[8]

While in the early days of the Gulfstream program the aircraft had been sold mainly within the United States, it was now branching out and

becoming a truly international product. To keep up with this change, Grumman American's marketing department, which was now headed up by Charles Vogeley, was split into two different areas covering international and domestic sales.

It was a period of growth, and once again record backlogs were making aviation news. *Aviation Week & Space Technology*, for instance, reported in September 1977:

> *"Record sales have driven business aircraft backlogs to new highs, and there is industry optimism that this strength will extend at least into 1980.... Grumman American said that it has firm orders for the Gulfstream II backlogged out to August 1978, which is the largest backlog it has had in several years. Previously the backlog has averaged eight or nine months of production."*[9]

Reengineering

Work on the new Gulfstream III design continued during the rising tide of sales and the festering feelings among the directors. The new GIII retained some of the advantages that, from the outset, were designed with the idea of retrofitting the GII. A new wing with winglets was retained from the original GIII design to boost fuel efficiency, along with the wraparound windshield, which improved visibility. The fuselage was extended by two feet rather than four feet.

The GIII was unique for Grumman Aerospace and its subsidiary because it was generated using computer-aided design, the first major project to use this important design tool at either company. "One of the proud accomplishments of the

Gulfstream III design team came from a source not derived from the airplane itself," noted the AIAA GIII case study written by engineers Charles Coppi, Lawrence Mead and John Strakosch. All of the master dimensions for the wing, winglet and wing/fuselage fairings were developed with the Grumman Engineering and Manufacturing System. The system was a company-wide tool, permitting the tooling and manufacturing departments direct access to the stored data.[10]

The study also stressed the teamwork demonstrated by engineers from Grumman American and Grumman Aerospace. The comment stood in stark contrast to Grumman American's board of directors. At that chilly meeting in New York, Bierwirth agreed to replace Corky Meyer, and in April 1978, Meyer resigned. Company officials candidly explained that his resignation was a concession to minority stockholders of Grumman American.

But Meyer's resignation was just the prelude to an even bigger change. And it began with a phone call out of the blue.

The revised GIII retained the winglets and added more wing area, but the supercritical wing was dropped. Each wing area encompassed 934 square feet, and the wings were swept back 28 degrees. *(Photo courtesy of Gulfstream Aerospace.)*

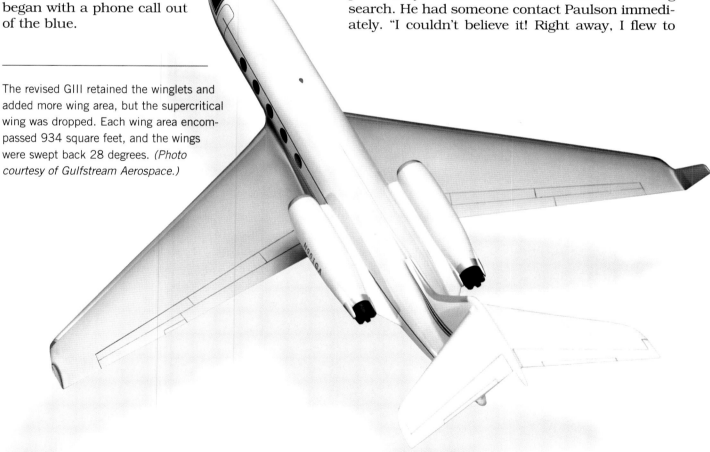

Under New Management

Shortly after Corky Meyer resigned, a man named Allen Paulson received a phone call from a Grumman Aerospace executive. Paulson, a self-made man who had risen from an airline mechanic for Trans World Airlines to become an aviation entrepreneur, had been looking for a place to build the Hustler 500, a unique two-engine airplane powered by a propeller in the front and a fanjet in the back, for more than a year.

"Word had gotten out among aviation publications that I was in the market to buy a company," Paulson said in an interview. He thought he had found the right place in Bethany, Oklahoma. The plant was owned by Rockwell International, and negotiations had just broken down because the five- to seven-passenger Hustler would have been competitive with Rockwell's own line of 690B Turbo Commanders. Terms were never reached. Meanwhile, Bierwirth, who had never met Paulson personally, read about Paulson's continuing search. He had someone contact Paulson immediately. "I couldn't believe it! Right away, I flew to

New York to meet with them," recalled Paulson. "We came up with a figure of about $52 million. We made a deal within three days."[11]

As Russ Meyer, the former CEO of Grumman American, noted: "My God, anybody in their right mind would be interested in buying Gulfstream."[12]

The agreement called for Grumman Aerospace to buy out the Cleveland Group. The minority shareholders had rejected Bierwirth's earlier buy-out offer of $5 a share, demanding instead $10 a share. At the February meeting, they wanted $8.50 a share, which, in the end, is what they received. Stunned by Bierwirth's move, Ingalls, Modell and Stranahan sold their interest for $17 million. According to Forbes, the amount was "at best, not much more than recouping their total investment."[13]

Selling the Gulfstream program left a wake of bad feelings and bitterness toward Bierwirth. Although it was just one of many programs for Grumman, Grummanites were proud of their civilian line known as "the Cadillac of the Sky" and flown by many of the best known, most powerful and most respected people in the world. More than 60 of the top corporations on the Fortune 500 list, for instance, were flying Gulfstreams, as did many heads of state by the time of the deal.

The terms were settled in late July, and the sale was complete. "It was a shock to everybody," recalled Bob Smyth, who at the time was director of flight test.

"On the Monday the sale of Gulfstream was announced, Jack Bierwirth came to lunch in the Grumman executive dining room in an adjacent restaurant known as the Farm House. Corporate directors took turns taking five or six of their employees to sit at the head table so the senior officers could meet them informally, and this day was my turn. When Jack sat down, he said, 'I guess you guys are going to be disappointed in what happened over the weekend, but believe me, I did it in the best interest of Grumman.' I thought that was baloney."[14]

The decision to sell off the Gulfstream program had an impact throughout Grumman as well, one that could still be felt after more than 20 years.

"Separating from Grumman was a traumatic experience for everybody," recalled Albert "Goldie" Glenn. "It left a bitter taste that hasn't gone away."[15]

Furthermore, few people had heard of Allen Paulson at the time. An article in Aviation International News that explored the sale was titled "AJI and Allen Who?"

"When Jimmy Carter was running for president, the wags where saying, 'Jimmy who?' Recently, at the announcement of the sale of Grumman American Aviation Corp. to American Jet Industries, the question 'AJI and Allen Who?' was making the rounds."[16]

However, the article concluded that, like Jimmy Carter, who would be known by the world, "Soon American Jet Industries and its president, Allen Paulson, will be as well known in general aviation circles as they are to those familiar with aircraft manufacturing and modifications."

Many analysts believe Bierwirth had no choice. Grumman's commitment to diversify meant it could not sustain Grumman American, which was losing money on its line of light planes. The holding company, Grumman Corporation, was building canoes, shipping containers, sailboats, fire engines, solar hot water heaters and so forth, along with providing computer services. About a month before it divested Grumman American, Grumman purchased Flxible Buses from Rohr Industries. It soon discovered that the buses suffered from structural defects; the division quickly lost money.

Others felt the move was necessary to allow Gulfstream the freedom to grow. "I don't think Jack Bierwirth today is liked very much for that," explained Herman Schonenberg, who was director of materials at the main plant in Bethpage, Long Island.

"But in the long run, if you look at it objectively, he did the right thing. At the time it didn't look right, but it worked to the benefit of the whole Gulfstream program. Those associated with the Gulfstream were able to get into a whole lot more, including making the interiors, which is very profitable. Allen Paulson is the type not to sit back; he sees something good, he jumps at it."[17]

Almost overnight Paulson's $40 million American Jet Industries became a $200 million company with the addition of Grumman American. Paulson purchased a company that was losing $2 million the year he bought it, and one with a dispirited workforce, but he had faced bigger challenges in his life.

Up by His Own Bootstraps

When Bierwirth had decided to sell Grumman American, he assigned Peter Viemeister, then vice president of development for Grumman Aerospace, the task of finding a suitable buyer. "My assignment was to help find a buyer for GAAC," Viemeister said, "and to do it discreetly, with no publicity, until a deal looked probable.

"Any leak or rumor could make it look like a desperation sale and cause Grumman stock to vacillate.... I went on a merry chase, following *leads from members of the Grumman board. I would visit the prospect, usually alone, to brief him and answer any questions."[18]*

This quest took him to Ivy League clubs, Park Avenue residences and even Denver, where he met with the head of an oil company.[19] Eventually, John Carr, then vice chairman of Grumman Aerospace, told Viemeister that he had a lead for him. He had been told that an enterprising former mechanic who now headed up his own aircraft company in California might be interested. His name was Allen Paulson. Viemeister remembered that, at the time, Paulson

---

Allen Paulson fell in love with aviation as a teenager watching airplanes take off from an airfield in San Francisco. He once took a ride with a barnstormer named Tex Rankin. *(Photo courtesy of Gulfstream Aerospace.)*

One of the chief reasons Paulson was interested in purchasing Gulfstream was to produce his pet project — the Hustler. An early version included a Pratt & Whitney turboprop engine in the nose and a turbofan engine in the tail. *(Photo courtesy of Bob Cooper.)*

was in his mid-fifties, tall, slightly balding, and had alert eyes and aristocratic bearing. He spoke calmly about his past and plans for the future.[20]

Allen Paulson was born in 1922 on a farm in Clinton, Iowa. He was the youngest of five boys. At age 13, he left home to seek his fortune. He supported himself through high school by taking odd jobs, such as selling newspapers and working as a janitor in a hotel. When he was 15, he played at bingo and won $100, which he used to buy a bus ticket to San Francisco. Working on a dairy farm, Paulson fell in love with flying by watching airplanes land and take off from a nearby airfield. One day, he took a ride with a barnstormer named Tex Rankin and was hooked.

Paulson took several college courses in engineering and eventually entered an airline mechanic training program offered by TWA's predecessor. When World War II broke out, he was earning 30 cents an hour as a TWA airline mechanic. Paulson joined the Army Air Corps to become a pilot, but he was kept on the field because of his experience as a mechanic.

After the war, Paulson used the money from his GI Bill to become a pilot. He went to work for TWA again, this time as flight technician for the four-engine Lockheed Constellation passenger aircraft. Paulson noticed that the Constellation's engines, which were prone to low oil pressure and cylinder failure, were not designed to distribute oil correctly. "The engines were experiencing a lot of cylinder failures, and we couldn't figure out why," Paulson said.

"I developed the theory that with the big counterweights going around, the pressure lubricated the upper cylinders but didn't get to the lower cylinders. I came up with a way to pressure lubricate the lower cylinders."[21]

During World War II, Paulson served as a flight mechanic in the U.S. Army Air Corps. Upon his discharge, he became a TWA flight engineer. In his off-hours, he tinkered with engines to find ways to improve them. *(Photo courtesy of Gulfstream Aerospace.)*

Paulson borrowed $1,500 from the company's credit union — his first real business risk — and purchased several surplus B-29 engines and began tinkering. He came up with the solution, which he offered to his employer, but it was turned down. "There's a thing known as NIH in many corporations, and that's called 'not invented here,' " he said in an interview. "For someone who was not in their engineering department to tell them how to fix their engine, they just didn't want to listen. It was a 'Don't confuse me with the facts' kind of thing."[22]

Paulson started a sideline business selling the modifications he developed to other airlines and, eventually, to TWA. "I found it hard to pass on the opportunity," he said. "Early in life I discovered there is no such thing as a lazy, lucky guy."[23]

By 1951, Paulson had left TWA and founded California Airmotive Corporation, which specialized in converting used passenger aircraft into cargo planes. The business grew quickly. One year, he had $100,000 in revenue, he said. The next, over $1 million. A *Newsweek* article dubbed him the "Used Airliner King" and pictured his parking lot at California Airmotive stacked nose to tail with more than 50 planes. The article stated that his ragtag fleet was made up of "the propeller-driven flagships of the 1950s, the rejects in the rush to the big jets with mini-skirted stewardesses." His customers weren't always in the field of aviation, however — firefighters in Los Angeles, for instance, bought scores of old airliner seats from Paulson to loll around in back at their fire stations.[24]

While not particularly glamorous, California Airmotive was lucrative. By 1969, the year the *Newsweek* article was published, the company was doing more than $14 million in sales of used aircraft and parts.

"During the last decade he has sold about 300 airplanes, including 110 Constellations at $35,000 to $95,000 each, a hundred DC-7s, also at $35,000 to $95,000 each, scores of the old DC-3 workhorses at $10,000 each and an assortment of Electras at nearly $1 million each. A recent purchase was Eastern Airlines' entire remaining fleet of 42 piston planes."[25]

Paulson also became a distributor for Learjet in 10 Western states, and soon he was the No. 1 dealer in the Learjet sales operation.

In 1967, Paulson had also founded American Jet Industries (AJI), which concentrated on con-

---

In 1967, Paulson founded American Jet Industries in Van Nuys, California. *(Photo courtesy of Bob Cooper.)*

verting propeller-driven aircraft to propjets. He merged California Airmotive with AJI in 1974. Not content with merely converting and repairing aircraft, Paulson designed one of his own, which he called the Hustler. Powered by a turboprop engine in the front and a fanjet in the rear, the Hustler could take off from a short runway using the prop and then switch to the jet once it achieved cruising altitude. The Hustler was able to cruise at 470 miles an hour.[26]

The Hustler would never be certified, but it changed Paulson's life profoundly because it attracted the attention of Gerald Henderson, a venture capitalist and an aviation buff — the best combination for AJI.

Henderson had been a transport pilot in the 1920s, and his enthusiasm for aviation never waned, even though he amassed his wealth from investing in Avon products and pioneering cable television on the West Coast. He learned how to fly a helicopter in 1977, when he was 72.[27]

Henderson was immediately enamored with the Hustler. He bought 45 percent interest in AJI, with the majority held by Paulson. In short, Henderson became a financial angel, and his involvement was crucial to the success of Paulson's purchase of Grumman American. "Henderson, like Paulson, is a loner," noted the *Washington Post*, "part of a vanishing breed of sole proprietors who do not have to justify their actions to stockholders or anyone else."[28]

With Henderson's backing, Paulson was able to conclude the deal and became CEO and president of the company. He secured the right to keep the Gulfstream name, and Grumman American became Gulfstream American.

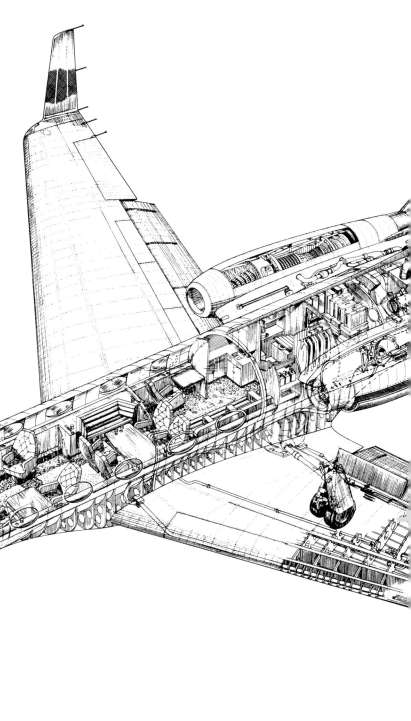

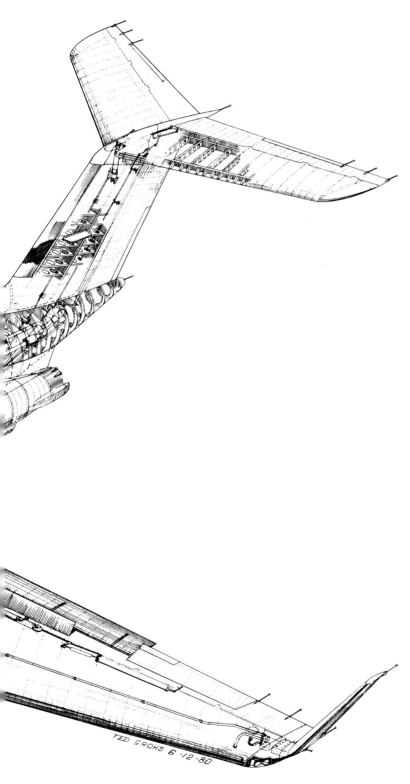

Setting Priorities

One of Paulson's priorities when he came aboard was getting the Hustler into production. Just after the purchase, Paulson explained that he hoped to have the aircraft certified in Van Nuys and then phase production into the Savannah facility.

"I am convinced this is going to be a very successful airplane and that we are going to sell a lot of them," he said at the time. "I wanted a company that would build it properly, and I believe I couldn't have found a better company."[29]

Another priority was the GIII. Soon after taking command, Paulson announced that the GIII development work was on schedule and the first flight was slated for November 1979 and certification would take place less than a year after that, noted *Aviation Week*.

"Gulfstream American is preparing for the production and certification of its Gulfstream III, Hustler 500 and Turbo AgCat, while dropping the two-place Lynx from its smaller single and multi-engine line for 1979."[30]

At the same time, Gulfstream was taking orders for a retrofit program to install the GIII's wings (complete with winglets) on Gulfstream II aircraft, and the last GII, number 258, was slated for delivery in early 1980.[31]

The close relationship between Grumman Aerospace and its former subsidiary continued on the GII program, but with a twist: Now Grumman Aerospace was the subcontractor, working for Gulfstream American. The aircraft was to be flight-tested at Grumman's test area on the south coast of Long Island, and members from both organizations were still able to work comfortably with each other. But Paulson had big plans to grow Gulfstream American far beyond what many people thought possible.

An illustration of the interior of the redesigned GIII. Test pilots noted that the GIII handled more gently in many respects than its predecessor. The GIII retained the previous Gulfstream's integral fuel tank design. *(Image courtesy of Gulfstream Aerospace.)*

Unlike its competition, Gulfstream soared during industry-wide downturns. *(Photo courtesy of Gulfstream Aerospace.)*

CHAPTER SIX

SOARING OVER OBSTACLES

1979–1982

"I saw the company come alive like you wouldn't believe. He let us do the job the way we knew we should."

— Dan Murphy, 1999[1]

L OOKING BACK AT THE immediate challenges faced by Allen Paulson in 1978, *Fortune* magazine wrote that "the most serious of the problems Paulson inherited was a dispirited sales force."[2] Paulson told the magazine writer that he saw that the organization had very good managers throughout the company, including in the sales force, but they needed momentum and leadership to provide that momentum.

Paulson's job was not made any easier by a rash of bad economic news in 1979 and the early 1980s. In fact, the beginning of the new decade looked suspiciously like the middle of the old decade. The cost of fuel was again rising, along with inflation and unemployment. The Federal Reserve Board, chaired by Paul Volcker, put the squeeze on borrowing by boosting interest rates a full percentage point. The historic measure was called the "Saturday Night Massacre" by the press because Volcker presented it during a rare Saturday night press conference.[3]

The series of recessions would wreak havoc on most general aviation companies, including Cessna, Piper and Beechcraft, which relied heavily on sales of small private airplanes. Sales of business jets did somewhat better, but the value of maintaining a corporate fleet was just too great. Even in 1982, the worst year of the recession, cor-

porations merely delayed the purchase of new aircraft. With three out of every four general aviation flight hours generated by business, corporations would no sooner give up their aircraft than get rid of their computing systems.[4]

In large part, the industry had the federal government to thank for the growing strength of business aviation. In 1979, the Airline Deregulation Act took effect, ending 40 years of federal protection for the airlines.[5] The act gave airlines the freedom to pull out of marginal routes, leaving those flights to commuter lines of questionable solvency. Freed from subsidies and oversight, airlines cut service to make ends meet, opening a gap that the general aviation industry rushed to fill.

Growing Gulfstream — A Little TLC

When it was part of Grumman Aerospace, Gulfstream was just another program — albeit a prestigious one — that had to compete for attention within a conservative, cost-conscious, multibillion-dollar corporation. Under Paulson, how-

---

As part of the company's marketing campaign, these envelopes were taken for a ride on the GIII's first flight and then sent to prospective GIII customers. *(Image courtesy of Joseph Anckner.)*

ever, it received loving care from someone who knew how to make money.

The year 1979 had started with all employees receiving a pay raise, a surefire way of improving morale for the short term. For the long term, Paulson began unshackling the Gulfstream program by giving his managers unprecedented freedom in ways that would fundamentally change the way the company dealt with customers. No longer did a decision have to crawl interminably up the chain of command. "I saw the company come alive like you wouldn't believe," reminisced retired Gulfstreamer Dan Murphy. "He let us do the job the way we knew we should."[6]

Bill Bauer agreed, adding that the links in an intolerably long chain of command were reduced to just one. "Before the sale, we had to clear everything first with Grumman," he said.

"We would have to make a big presentation in New York and then wait months for an answer. With Mr. Paulson, he liked it or he didn't like it. If he liked it, you were on your way with the OK."[7]

For instance, Gulfstream immediately launched plans to expand into the lucrative area of aircraft completions. Unlike Grumman's management, which abhorred the idea of completing interiors and exteriors, Paulson had no qualms about indulging the whim of any customer of the Gulfstream, and neither did his crew. In August 1979, the company broke ground on a 116,000-square-foot completion center and a 12,400-square-foot paint hangar. Construction got off to a shaky start when Hurricane David hit two weeks after work began and almost wiped out what was accomplished, but by 1980 the center was running.[8] Further expansion was planned.

The $4 million completion center eventually gave Gulfstream American the ability to finish or refurbish the interiors and exteriors of the com-

Gulfstream American
Southern exposure

VOLUME 6, NUMBER 2   SAVANNAH, GEORGIA   APRIL 25, 1980

President's Message

In view of the time which has elapsed since my last report to you on the Gulfstream III, it seems appropriate to bring you up-to-date.

You will recall that the first Gulfstream III, Serial No. 249, was delivered to Grumman in December, 1979, under the terms of our contract with Grumman to test and obtain FAA certification.

The Gulfstream has performed admirably under all tests performed to date. The tests completed at this point indicate close adherence to the predicted performance in terms of speed, altitude and efficiency. It has actually been flown to a Mach number of .92, well beyond its most efficient cruise speed of .775 (about 445 knots at cruise altitude). A maximum altitude of 45,000 feet has also been achieved. During this period, the Gulfstream has been remarkably free of day-to-day mechanical difficulties.

Gulfstream III #2, Serial No. 252, was delivered to Grumman on January 2, 1980, for use in the required static proof load test portion of the program. Tests actually started on March 10 and are expected to be complete in mid- to late-April. These tests will ensure that there is adequate strength in the wings, winglets and empennage.

Fatigue tests are required on the forward fuselage, since that is an area of major change. An appropriate test article was delivered to Grumman on February 8. The necessary "bird impact" tests on the windshield were completely successful, and the 40,000 cycle fatigue test will start in April.

We anticipate clearance by the end of

OUTFITTING CENTER NEARS COMPLETION

In August 1979 Gulfstream American broke ground on what is to be a 116,000 square foot outfitting completion center for Gulfstream Aircraft. The $4,000,000 investment is designed to give the company the capability to completely finish interiors and exteriors of new Gulfstream III's and also refurbish interiors and exteriors of existing aircraft.

The construction got off to a shaky start with hurricane "David" hitting us two weeks after work began and almost wiped out what was accomplished. ARAMCO Construction was able to make up most of the lost time and construction should be completed by June 16. When the building is done Gulfstream American will be able to outfit 8 aircraft at one time. In addition to the 60,000 square feet of hangar area, the building will have 56,000 square feet of shop and office area. These areas will have custom design engineering, custom avionics, bench test, upholstery and trim shop, cabinet, and sheetmetal shops.

In addition to the outfitting completion center construction effort is going forward on a new paint hangar which will give the company capability to do exterior paint work on Gulfstream size aircraft. The 12,400 square foot building should be completed July 30, 1980. The company believes this investment will be very advantageous by expanding our capabilities in providing our customers a fully completed quality aircraft. This investment will also provide more security and growth for our employees.

April to commence testing with the FAA on board and certification by the end of July.

The sales picture on the Gulfstream III continues to be very strong. Firm contracts have been signed for 57 air-planes. Additional contracts for 4 are presently being negotiated. Assuming that all of the latter are successfully completed, we are sold out through October, 1982.

plete Gulfstream line. Up to eight aircraft could be worked on at the same time.[9]

"The center's designers don't blink when a sheikh or chief executive requests an elaborate stereo system, a video game console, a private bedroom or a fancy bathtub," noted *Fortune* magazine writer Kenneth Labich in a May 1983 issue. "Last month, workers at the center were outfitting a European businessman's Gulfstream III with gold-plated bathroom fixtures."[10]

In an article in *Aviation Week & Space Technology*, Allen Paulson discussed the changes taking place in the company during this period: "Gulfstream is trying to become completely self-sufficient for parts and take on more programs," he said.[11]

Under Grumman, the company installed just enough avionics to fly the airplane to a completion center, where state-of-the-art equipment would then be installed. Paulson insisted that Gulfstream American offer a customized avionics package. The company had always wanted to be a "one-stop shop" for Gulfstream customers. Offering completions was another service to make this a reality.

"The company believes this investment will be very advantageous by expanding our capabilities in providing our customers a fully completed quality aircraft," explained an article in *Southern Exposure*, the company newsletter. "This investment will also provide more security and growth for our employees."[12]

There was another advantage to the "one-stop shop" method: Gulfstream American employees could better advise customers on achieving a balance between a desired customized interior and

Allen Paulson launched an ambitious expansion program to begin outfitting aircraft with interiors and avionics, areas Grumman Aerospace had resisted for years. *(Image courtesy of Gulfstream Aerospace.)*

the corresponding trade-off in reduction of either fuel or passengers.

In keeping with this philosophy, the company also started direct sales instead of subcontracting sales to outside distributors, which had been the practice until this time.

Up and Away

During the official Gulfstream III rollout ceremonies, attended by about 500 dignitaries and employees, Allen Paulson referred to the latest Gulfstream as "the new definition of the ... fastest and largest range corporate airplane in the world ... and the queen of our business fleet."[13]

Ribbons were cut by several attending dignitaries including Gulfstream customers Drummond Bell, chairman of the board of National Distillers & Chemical Corporation, and representatives of the Danish air force, along with Georgia Governor George Busbee.[14]

Aviation International News noted that "Gulfstream III's rollout at Savannah ... not only marked the beginning of an era of business jets with ranges beyond 3,600 nautical miles, it also broke the $10 million barrier for a completed airplane."[15]

Indeed, the range of the GIII was 3,760 nautical miles with eight passengers and baggage, while the long-range cruise was Mach .775 and the maximum fuel capacity 27,900 pounds.[16]

On December 2, 1979, out of Savannah, the GIII made its first flight. A total of four flights were made in Savannah. Because the design was so similar to that of the second Gulfstream, the first flight was actually made by a converted GII. On December 11, the airplane was ferried to Grumman Aerospace's excellent flight test facility in Calveston, Long Island, to enter the flight test program. After it sold Grumman American to Paulson, Grumman Aerospace became a subcontractor and worked in cooperation with Gulfstream American. According to the agreement, each company supplied a test pilot for the Gulfstream program. Gulfstream assigned test pilot Morgan Cobb, while Bob Smyth, still with Grumman at this point, continued his work with the Gulfstream program.

The original price of the first 10 airplanes was $7.4 million each. The cost did not include an interior but did include standard avionics — Sperry's SPZ-800 autopilot — along with a flight direction and air data system, weather radar and navigational computer.[17]

The first flight went smoothly, but the aircraft did little except take off, climb to about 25,000 feet, and then land. Smyth said the real work begins not with the first flight but with the second. "For the first flight, you have the press and a lot of dignitaries on hand to watch. So the most important thing is to make a good landing, get the thing on the ground and then have fun at the party," he said. "It doesn't matter, really, how much you've accomplished on that first time out."[18]

A true prototype — built from the ground up as a GIII — made its first flight on December 24.

During the first flight of the GIII, pilots were cautious about pushing the aircraft too hard. It did little more than take off, climb to a low cruising altitude and land smoothly.

Overall, the GIII was very similar to the GII in terms of handling. The GIII, with its larger wing span and wingtips, provided more lateral inertia than the GII. Pilots of the GII had reported that they tended to overcontrol when they put the full flap down, but the GIII was more gentle in that respect.

The wing area for the GIII had been increased from 800 square feet to 934 square feet for each wing. The wings were swept back 28 degrees, more than the GII, and retained the GII's proven integral fuel tank design. Besides better lift, the larger wing span provided 4,600 more pounds of fuel than the GII, boosting the GIII's range. If time was of the essence, the GIII could cross the United States, from east to west, at Mach .84 and land on the West Coast one hour earlier than the GII. The GIII, with its winglets, was also more fuel efficient. At a long-range cruise speed of Mach .775, the GIII used 23 percent less fuel than the GII. The final fuel capacity of the GIII was 28,300 pounds, which was 5,000 pounds more than the GII's.

The Spey engines from the GII were kept because they were well matched to the GIII's long-range economy cruise speed. "The normal cruising airspeed of the aircraft occurs in this power range — well below the maximum cruise power rating of the engine," noted a GIII engineering case study.

"Consequently, the aircraft has a fairly wide latitude in power availability to enable it to cater to unanticipated situations. The ability to alter airspeed or change altitude or adjust for wind conditions results in a very 'real world' forgiveness factor that ensures trip completion and schedule adherence."[19]

The Spey had the further advantage of longevity and reliability. The engines, on average, required routine overhaul every 7,000 hours, and history had shown that the average annual use of the Gulfstream was about 700 hours. Under those conditions, the engines required overhaul every 10 years.

The overall length of the wings remained the same as the GI, which meant that GIII operators wouldn't have to move to a bigger hangar.

In the fuselage, a wraparound windshield offered better visibility because it reduced the number of support posts. The design also reduced cockpit noise at cruising speeds because it guarded against separated flow conditions arising from the use of angled windshield posts.

Two feet were added just aft of the main entrance door, providing more storage volume. The nose was lengthened for aesthetic reasons only and did not change the aircraft's aerodynamic performance.

Breaking Records

The FAA certified the Gulfstream III for production in September 1980. By that time, the GIII had shattered a number of records. The third production Gulfstream, N300GA, set two World Class records in April 1980 when Allen Paulson and Bob Smyth flew nonstop from Savannah to Hanover, West Germany — a distance of 4,569 miles — in just eight hours and 58 minutes. The aircraft then went on display at Hanover's 1980 International Air Show.

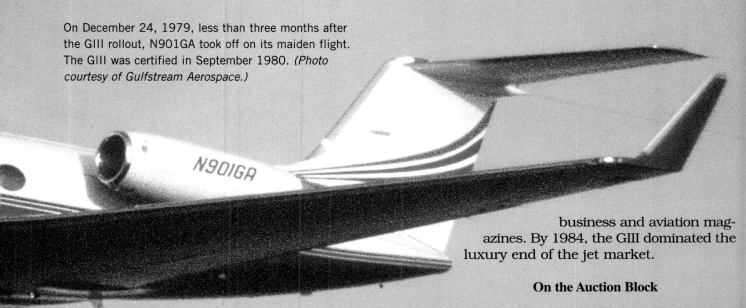

On December 24, 1979, less than three months after the GIII rollout, N901GA took off on its maiden flight. The GIII was certified in September 1980. *(Photo courtesy of Gulfstream Aerospace.)*

business and aviation magazines. By 1984, the GIII dominated the luxury end of the jet market.

On the Auction Block

Upon his arrival at the show, Paulson released a statement to aviation writers: "We are very pleased to have established these records because they clearly demonstrate the advanced performance of our new Gulfstream III.

"We have achieved our target of a 30 percent increase in range and a higher cruising speed compared with the Gulfstream II. Our order book for nearly 60 of these aircraft shows the confidence of our customers in this latest version of the Gulfstream."[20]

A month later, the GIII set a civilian jet altitude record when it climbed to more than 52,000 feet. After that, the GIII broke another distance record when it flew 5,005 miles nonstop from Japan to Los Angeles.[21] Besides its distance, speed and altitude records, the GIII won distinction during a record-setting flight in November 1983 by becoming the first business jet to fly over both poles.

Setting records was one of Paulson's imaginative ways to grab attention, headlines and, ultimately, orders. The records showed the reliability of the engineering and the confidence the pilots and passengers had in the Gulfstream on long nonstop flights.

With or without these records, the GIII simply outclassed every jet in its category, according to

After he took charge of the company, Paulson quickly decided to do away with the line of light planes. They had never made a profit, and the recession was proving disastrous for companies dependent upon light pleasure aircraft. Paulson also wanted to make room for the various development and production programs in the works or on the drawing boards. In May 1979, the light aircraft line was put on the auction block.

At the time, the company's light aircraft lineup included the twin-engine GA-7 Cougar, AA-5A Cheetah and AA-5B Tiger. Since deliveries began in early 1978, 115 of the four-seat Cougar aircraft had been built. Due to Paulson's decision, production was expected to stop that summer on the Cougar, while production of the single-engine AA-5A Cheetah and AA-5B Tiger would stop in December. Production of two versions of the company's two-place aircraft had stopped the previous year.[22]

"The Cheetah, Tiger and Cougar are well-built aircraft and will outperform anything in their weight and power category but they do not fit in with our goals," Paulson said.[23] Bob Coman, who was the program manager for the light aircraft product line, explained that they were "great, great airplanes, but we were really in a sense losing money on each airplane."[24]

In addition, the company was negotiating with the Schweizer Aircraft Corporation of Elmira, New York, to purchase Gulfstream's AgCat agri-

Paulson put the light aircraft segment of Gulfstream on the auction block. He had inherited the lines when he bought the company, but they were not turning a profit. *(Photo courtesy of Gulfstream Aerospace.)*

cultural aircraft. Although the aircraft was a part of the company's aircraft offerings, it was never actually produced in Savannah. It was built at Schweizer.

"We plan to sell the whole program, and I do not see any great changes to the aircraft when we do,'" Paulson told *Aviation Week* about the sale.[25]

Stretching the Gulfstream I

With the light aircraft programs up for sale, Gulfstream tried to stretch the market for the original Gulfstream. It was a valiant attempt to capitalize on the growing commuter airliner segment, which was springing up as the major airlines cut back on service to less-profitable routes. In September 1979, Gulfstream American announced the introduction a stretched version of the GI, to be designated the GI-C, to be used as a commuter aircraft.[26] "We decided we would stretch the Gulfstream I ... and see what the market would do," said Bob Coman. Coman had moved from light aircraft to become the program manager for the GI-C.[27]

To lengthen the airplane, the fuselage was cut into two pieces. A 72-inch extension was inserted just forward of the wing, and a 56.5-inch extension was inserted just aft of the wing. This extended the fuselage by some 10 feet. As a result, passenger capacity doubled as the number of seats increased from 19 to 38.[28]

The first flight of the GI-C was on October 25, 1980. The initial flights raised some concerns because the aircraft was initially hard to handle. "It's a marvelously robust airplane," described engineer Ed Flinn, who worked on the project. "But it can be pretty demanding." Flinn said the modified aircraft tended to track in an unintended direction on landing.

The FAA approved the modified design, and the GI-C was the first major certification program performed entirely by Gulfstream American.[29]

Air North, a commuter airline based in Burlington, Vermont, received the first GI-C, to be used in daily operations on two of the commuter airline's major routes serving Rochester, Washington and Boston. Prior to delivery, the aircraft was displayed along with 20 other aircraft at the Commuter Airline Association meeting in Phoenix, Arizona.[30]

The first two GI-Cs were built in Savannah, but then production was moved off-site to a company in Alabama, where an additional three were built.[31] Gulfstream had intended to set up a production line to build the GI-C from scratch.[32]

The program stopped after the fifth GI-C was built, however. The recessive economy was not friendly to commuter airlines because of the high cost to operate a smaller aircraft. Furthermore, after a short hiatus, the major airlines began a limited return to short-haul feeds from the most lucrative markets, and passengers preferred jets to "puddle jumpers."[33]

Finally, the members of Gulfstream's marketing department were not enthusiastic about the GI-C. They were used to dealing one-on-one with the chairmen and CEOs of major corporations, in which ability to pay was not generally a concern. Trying to sell a GI-C to a small, struggling regional airline was a different matter. "Owners of small airlines wanted us to tell them where they could get the money to pay for an airplane," Coman explained. "We weren't built that way."

Air North was the first customer for the Gulfstream I-C, a stretched version of the GI. Only five were built. *(Photo courtesy of Gulfstream Aerospace.)*

"We never made the commitment to go back in and build that airplane. But we learned from it. We learned that we really didn't want to get into the regional airliner business."[34]

Tesoro Petroleum: A Marriage Never Consummated

Meanwhile, Paulson and Gerald Henderson, the wealthy aviation enthusiast who helped Paulson buy the company, were disagreeing frequently on business strategy. Paulson wanted to buy Henderson out. In January 1980, he found someone willing to help him: Tesoro Petroleum Corporation of

Allen Paulson placed emphasis on capturing speed and distance records to publicize the performance of the Gulfstream III. *(Photo courtesy of Gulfstream Aerospace.)*

San Antonio, Texas. Tesoro agreed in principle to buy Henderson's share of the company in a stock swap valued at $125 million. According to the agreement, Paulson would retain his position and his staff, and Grumman Aerospace would retain its shares of preferred stock.

Tesoro Petroleum began in 1964 when a man named Robert West purchased a small group of oil-producing properties and then went on an acquisition spree. "Tesoro became a hodgepodge of business interests," noted *Business Week*. "Gasoline marketing in California, a refinery in Alaska, oil equipment rental and manufacturing, contract drilling, oil transportation and production, even coal mining."[35]

A Tesoro senior vice president explained that "Gulfstream simply appeared to be available at a good price, even though unconnected to the oil business."[36] What made it so attractive to an energy company was its ability to generate cash.

The deal was never consummated, however. The oil industry was soon to experience turmoil as oil prices began a spectacular and devastating — from the oil industry's perspective — plunge. In addition, Paulson had secured financing elsewhere. Both sides agreed to call off the merger. In any case, Paulson was able to line up investors to buy out Henderson's stake.

To Build or Not to Build

Paulson was still searching for a place to build the Hustler 500, the aircraft that had so interested Henderson in the first place.

"It was a novel idea," said Bob Cooper, who was vice president of marketing for Gulfstream. "You had a twin-engine airplane when you needed one and a single engine airplane for economy."[37] Paulson had secured 76 refundable deposits for the Hustler by the time he completed the purchase of Grumman American. The program suffered a number of delays, however, as Gulfstream American workers concentrated on the GIII program. By May 1981, a Hustler prototype had logged just 30 hours of test time, and all of the deposits made on the aircraft were returned at the request of customers.

Another reason the program was delayed was because Gulfstream American had designed a derivative of the Hustler, which the company hoped would be accepted by the Air Force as a training aircraft. Called the Peregrine 600, the aircraft featured a side-by-side seating arrangement and was powered by a single rear-mounted Pratt & Whitney turbofan engine capable of producing 2,500 pounds of thrust.

The Peregrine was being developed in response to a request for bids for the Air Force's "Next

In 1981, Gulfstream produced the GII-B, a GII fitted with wings and winglets from the GIII. The airplane first took flight on March 17, 1981. *(Photo courtesy of Gulfstream Aerospace.)*

The Hustler gradually lost favor as Paulson's pet project. He eventually decided against it altogether.

Generation Trainer," or "NGT," to replace the Air Training Command's aging fleet of Cessna T-37 jets. The first flight took place in Oklahoma in early 1982.

The Peregrine went through several different designs, including one version featuring either tandem or side-by-side seating and powered by either a single tail-mounted Pratt & Whitney JT 15D-5 engine or a pair of 1,500-pound thrust fanjets mounted conventionally on the rear of the fuselage. In another version, the Peregrine NGT was powered by two Williams International FJ44 turbofans with the engines mounted inside the fuselage to reduce drag and increase performance.[38]

As the design took shape, Paulson considered dropping the Hustler altogether in favor of a business version of the Peregrine, one powered by twin rear-mounted engines, each producing 1,200 pounds of thrust. "The Peregrine appears to be a better airplane than the Hustler from the standpoint of performance and economy, and that's the name of the game today," he told *Aviation Week* in 1981.[39]

As he decided on the fate of the Hustler, Paulson began negotiations again with Rockwell International to buy its plant in Bethany, Oklahoma. Almost three years earlier, Paulson and Rockwell were unable to come to terms for the purchase of Bethany, where Paulson had originally hoped to

build the Hustler. However, the Hustler and Rockwell's Commander 700, which was being built in cooperation with Japan's Fuji Jet Industries, would have competed against one another.

The situation was different in 1981. Fuji and Rockwell had terminated their agreement several months earlier, and in February Gulfstream American bought the Bethany operation, which had a large pool of labor and an in-house FAA certification facility. By the time the deal was completed, Paulson had decided to drop the Hustler entirely in favor of a corporate version of the Peregrine. Renamed the Commander Business Aircraft Division of Gulfstream American, the division continued production of three models of turboprop aircraft — the 840, 980 and 1000.[40]

About the purchase, Paulson said, "The Commander aircraft product support will continue in full force through our Gulfstream Commander ServiCenters network. We intend to continue to improve our position in the jetprop segment of the general aviation market, and our worldwide distribution and support operations are important contributors to that improvement."[41] With the purchase, Gulfstream American had approximately 3,500 employees and 1.7 million square feet of facilities.

Gulfstream lost out in the competition to produce a military trainer. The Peregrine's military applications were abandoned in favor of developing a business transport. It wasn't long before economic conditions put an end to the Peregrine entirely.[42]

Bucking the Trend

As the recession continued, Gulfstream began seeing new orders fall. In 1981, customers ordered 32 Gulfstreams, but a year later only 15 new orders were received.

Despite a drop in the number of airplanes sold, Gulfstream American continued to grow in manufacturing space and in employees, unlike many of its competitors. Seemingly recession-proof, Gulfstream owned the high-end of the business jet market. With no real competition, the company could prosper because its customers looked at their corporate fleets as vital business tools rather than expendable luxuries.

Below: In 1980, Gulfstream purchased the Bethany, Oklahoma, plant where Rockwell's Commander line of aircraft was built. Shown below is the Commander manufacturing line.

Inset: A marketing brochure for the Commander jetprop. The line was continued after its acquisition.
(Images courtesy of Albert Glenn.)

By 1981, the Hustler was no longer being developed as a corporate aircraft but as a flying test bed for the Peregrine 600 corporate aircraft (left) and a military trainer (right). Neither program got off the ground. *(Images courtesy of Bob Cooper.)*

In December 1981, Gulfstream officials announced a two-year expansion. The plan called for the hiring of several hundred people in 1982 and 1983.[43] An article in the *Savannah News-Press* in March 1982 noted that the company "continues its growth in the face of the economic recession. Paulson heads a team of more than 3,500 employees — about 2,500 here in Savannah. The total number of employees stood at only 1,996 at the end of 1980."[44]

Meanwhile, the GIII was continuing to make headlines. In 1982, a GIII achieved an around-the-world record. *The Spirit of America*, owned and operated by National Distillers & Chemical Corporation, departed New Jersey's Teterboro Airport on January 8 and covered a total of 23,314.55 statute miles in a record-breaking time of 47 hours, 39 minutes and 3 seconds. The flight beat the previous record of 57 hours and 25 minutes set by golfer Arnold Palmer in a Learjet in 1976.[45]

As 1982 drew to a close, Paulson once again changed the name of the company. In November, Gulfstream American became Gulfstream Aerospace Corporation.

In a message to employees, Allen Paulson explained the reason the name was evolving once again:

*"The new name will broaden the scope of Gulfstream's dealings with the entire world since over 60 percent of our sales are currently world-wide compared to past overseas sales of 40 percent. We are proud of our American heritage. However, "American" in our company name did not reflect our product. Since our company product image is expanding in scope ... we feel Aerospace announced to the world our future technological goals."[46]

For the C-20 rollout, a color guard stood at formal parade rest and a band played "Off We Go Into the Wild Blue Yonder." *(Photo courtesy of Bob Coman.)*

CHAPTER SEVEN

IN THE PUBLIC EYE

1982–1985

*"Gulfstream Aerospace has long mystified business aircraft manufac-
turers, who have wracked their brains trying to figure out what GA is
doing right, bucking seemingly implacable market trends and painting its
books with great slathers of black ink."*

— *Dun's Business Month*, 1986[1]

IN DECEMBER 1982, ALLEN
Paulson sat down with Ralph
Robins, the managing director for
Rolls-Royce, at a Christmas luncheon
held at the Waldorf-Astoria in New
York. After brief pleasantries, the con-
versation turned to the latest generation
of Gulfstreams — the Gulfstream IV.

The GIV project had just been publicly
announced, and engineers were wrestling with the
mission they knew the airplane had to fill — a
range of at least 4,000 nautical miles and greater
cruising speed, but with less noise and lower emissions than put out by the Spey engines. When
they originally conceived the GIV early in 1982,
engineers believed the aircraft would need four
engines, a prospect they dreaded.

Concurrently, Rolls-Royce was at work developing a turbofan engine capable of powering an
airliner more than twice the size of the GIV. The
proposed engine, called the Tay, was being designed
from scratch to meet more stringent regulations
that were to go into effect in 1984. Only two of the
powerful Tays would be needed to do the same
job as the four smaller engines and still meet federal environmental standards.

Although the engine wasn't being developed
with the GIV in mind, it was a perfect match for
the airplane. Rolls-Royce's engineers knew this
and called Gulfstream Chief Engineer Charles
Coppi to tell him about the Tay. After reviewing
the data, Coppi embarked on a cam-
paign to persuade Paulson that the
Tay was the right engine for the GIV.

The aviation recession by this time
had become an industry depression.
One aviation magazine called 1982
a "smelly, rabid, dig-up-the-flowers dog
of a year," which many in the industry
probably considered an understatement.[2] The
effects would linger throughout the decade.

Rolls-Royce had been particularly hard hit.
Lockheed's decision to phase out its L-1011 Tristar
and the general global decline in aircraft orders
forced the venerable British manufacturer to lay
off tens of thousands of people. In 1979, Rolls
employed more than 60,000 people; by 1982, the
company had been forced to reduce its workforce
to 47,000, with more layoffs on the way.[3]

Meanwhile, Coppi had persuaded Paulson that
the Tay was the right choice. When he sat with
Robins, Paulson was keenly interested in the power
plant. The engineering details had been worked out
over a period of months. The actual deal took less

The patch signifying Gulfstream's membership in the C-20
military aircraft program. In 1983, the GIII was selected to
serve as a special mission aircraft for the president, vice
president and other high officers of the U.S. government.
(Patch courtesy of Gulfstream Aerospace.)

than 10 minutes. "We wrote the essentials down on a napkin," recalled Robins, "the engine price, quantity, payment terms, but the ink was running. Someone sitting near us said if we were going to do a deal, we should have a piece of paper. He passed across a little card."[4]

Fifteen minutes later, Sir Ralph Robins had an initial order for 200 Tay engines — enough for 100 aircraft. Paulson left with a napkin, upon which the price for the engines was settled at $300 million.

In the lore of business, stories abound of multimillion-dollar deals being made on the backs of napkins. Most are at best apocryphal. In the case of the Tay engine for the GIV, however, both men have the evidence hanging framed in their respective offices.[5]

The details were formally settled in March 1983. Rolls-Royce began its long climb back to profitability, and Gulfstream had the key ingredient of the GIV business jet.

Going Public

The $300 million deal meant Gulfstream needed capital. To help pay for the development of the GIV, Paulson decided to take Gulfstream Aerospace public. It was an audacious move in light of the industry depression. But unlike the rest of the aviation industry, Gulfstream Aerospace was prosperous. Its growth in revenue and income was near the top of its industry, and market surveys had shown great interest in a fourth Gulfstream.

In April 1983, a month after Gulfstream committed to purchasing the engines, the company made history by offering 8.8 million shares to the public. It was the largest offering since the Ford Motor Company went public in 1956. The IPO, which started at $19 a share, sold out within the day. Paulson personally sold 4.7 million shares but still retained more than 70 percent of the stock.[6] "I have the best of both worlds," he told the *New York Times* shortly after the IPO. "I still have control of the company."[7]

Following the sale, Paulson shared the good fortune with Gulfstream's 3,500 workers by offering each employee 50 shares of stock.[8] "This is a token of my sincere thanks to all of you," Paulson told his workers. "You are now part owners of the greatest aviation company in the world."[9]

Bags are loaded onto the *American Dream II*, the GIII that would break a round-the-world record. Piloted by Brooke Knapp, the GIII flew over the North and South poles in November 1983. Knapp became the first female pilot to circumnavigate the globe. *(Photo courtesy of Bob Smyth.)*

Workers initially reacted with skepticism when the stock was offered. The term "IPO" was not part of the lexicon of the shop floor, and few employees had any experience with the stock market. "They didn't understand it then," said Albert Glenn, then the chief operating officer. "They thought, 'Gee whiz, maybe I'm now liable somehow.'"[10]

But it wasn't long before employees got over their initial concerns about owning a growing enterprise, and they were proud to be in the public eye, able to track their company's progress on the New York Stock Exchange.

Going public meant that Gulfstream Aerospace's performance during 1982, the worst year of the recession, was open for the public to examine. Investors who did their homework discovered that Gulfstream earned an impressive $43 million on revenues of $582 million, even during a period of depressed oil prices that hurt two major customers of corporate aircraft — Arab nations and international energy companies.[11]

On June 23, 1983, the 100th Gulfstream III rolled out of the Savannah facility. Remarking on the occasion in the company newsletter, *Southern Exposure*, Glenn said:

> *"Each of us realizes that no one person or one group of persons can claim the responsibility for the success of this or any other Gulfstream; it is truly the product of our entire Gulfstream family working as a team to produce the world's finest corporate jet."*[12]

Last but Certainly Not Least

Meanwhile, the GIII was flying high. Pilot Brooke Knapp broke a round-the-world record in November 1983 by flying a GIII over the North and South poles, averaging 334 miles an hour.

This and other records helped Gulfstream to secure orders from the Royal Danish air force, which ordered three modified aircraft to be used for maritime surveillance, air-sea rescue, and fishery patrol and protection. The airplanes would cover more than 210,000 square miles around Greenland, which is part of the Kingdom of Denmark, as well as more than 110,000 square miles around the Faeroe Islands, "a region so great that in bad weather a flight of over 900 miles to the nearest airfield might be necessary," noted aviation writer Michael Hardy.[13]

Gulfstream's greatest military honor came when the Air Force selected the GIII for its C-20 project,

Above: The C-20 military contract was a huge boon to Gulfstream. Under the contract, the government committed to seven GIIIs with the option for more. Here, government officials and military officers tour a GIII under construction. *(Photo courtesy of Bob Coman.)*

Below: The GIII was selected by the Royal Danish air force for its famous Squadron 721. The squadron routinely patrols tens of thousands of square miles over the North Atlantic, flying in high winds and from landing strips that are little more than stretches of gravel. The 721's motto is "Anytime, anywhere." *(Photo courtesy of Gulfstream Aerospace.)*

also known as C-SAM ("Special Air Mission). The C-20s were part of the 89th Military Airlift Wing, and C-SAM is the designation for a special-mission airplane to transport the president, vice president, members of the military high command and other high government officials.

The contract called for seven short-range and long-range aircraft. With aerospace behemoths Boeing and Lockheed competing, the contract was hotly contested. More than 30 different types of airplanes vied for the prestige — and the dollars — of serving in the 89th. The winner would supply the aircraft and maintain the equipment.[14]

The GIII matched all of the range requirements and then some. There was a hitch, however. The airplane had to be able to take off at a variety of short-field runways, often under 3,500 feet, which was below the GIII's rating. When Gulfstream engineer Ed Flinn saw the Request for Proposal

(RFP) from the Air Force, he immediately realized that the GIII's specifications could not match the RFP specifications. "I told Mr. Coppi, 'We're not in the hunt here,'" recalled Flinn. "What Grumman certified did not represent the capabilities from a performance perspective."

At the time, the testing and certification still took place at Grumman's test field in Calverton, Long Island. To recertify the aircraft in time for the bidding, Gulfstream's engineers did something unprecedented. Within 90 days, they managed to completely recertify the takeoff and landing-field lengths, shortening them by as much as 500 feet.

Charles Coppi said they were able to accomplish this feat because Gulfstream has always maintained a strong relationship with the FAA, never pushing or cajoling the agency to speed up its process. Gulfstream's engineers respected the job the FAA officers had to perform, and in return the FAA developed a good working relationship with the company. In fact, a number of Gulfstream's engineers were selected to act as FAA-designated engineering representatives. In these cases, the engineer wears the badge of the FAA, performing the tests and evaluations that would ultimately be used to certify the aircraft. Such a designation comes only after years of trust between the agency and the engineer.

In the case of the GIII, the FAA agreed to check the aircraft during the process, which was done in Mojave, California. In June, with the recertification complete, Charles Coppi and Allen Paulson traveled to Washington, D.C., for the presentation. Of more than 30 contestants, they were last in line, waiting for their turn in a room that was not well air-conditioned. Paulson and Coppi didn't get a chance to present the GIII until after 4 p.m., a time of day that is less than optimum for attention spans, especially in a hot, stuffy room.[15]

They presented three options. The first two matched many of the aircraft shown during the day — one aircraft specifically for long-range missions and one specifically meant for short-range missions. Then they showed the GIII, one aircraft that could perform both missions at ranges exceeding those of the other contestants while retaining short-field performance. Gulfstream won hands-down.

"It was a real coup," said Bob Coman, who was director of the C-20 program.[16] Along with the seven aircraft, which were to be leased and then pur-

Gulfstream was competing against 30 other contestants for the Air Force's C-SAM contract, but the company easily won. The GIII matched the government's requirements for a long-range aircraft while retaining short-field performance. *(Photo courtesy of Gulfstream Aerospace.)*

chased over seven years, the Air Force contracted with Gulfstream for logistical support at Andrews Air Force Base in Maryland and Ramstein Air Base in Germany.[17] Allen Paulson noted that the "full potential of the contract, if all options are exercised, would be valued at approximately $300 million."[18]

Paulson noted in the company newsletter that the contract's significance went beyond the immediate financial benefit:

"The selection of the Gulfstream III to provide special transportation for the president, world leaders and military officials is a strong endorsement of the aircraft by the United States Air Force. This endorsement will establish new avenues for Gulfstream to market the aircraft internationally."[19]

In September 1983, the Air Force took delivery of the first C-20A GIII. During the rollout ceremony at Gulfstream, a color guard stood at formal parade rest as a band played "Off We Go Into the Wild Blue Yonder." Those in attendance included Senator Sam Nunn of Georgia; Dr. Thomas Cooper, assistant secretary of the Air Force for research, development and logistics; Lieutenant General Robert Coverdale, vice commander in chief of the Military Airlift Command; and Brigadier General Elbert Harbour, the deputy of Airlift and Training Systems of the Aeronautical Systems Division.[20]

The majority of those in attendance at the ceremony were employees of Gulfstream Aerospace and their families. In an emotional tribute to the employees who made the aircraft possible, Allen Paulson noted, "I don't know about all of you, but it gives me goosebumps. To see the words 'United States of America' on the side of our airplane really makes me proud."[21]

Besides its VIP purpose, Gulfstream also outfitted the GIII to play a role similar to the one it per-

A Gulfstream C-20 in flight. Allen Paulson said that seeing "United States of America" emblazoned on a Gulfstream gave him goosebumps. *(Photo courtesy of* Air Force Magazine.*)*

formed for the Danish air force — maritime patrol, electronic surveillance and reconnaissance. Designated the SRA-1, the aircraft was modified so its interior could be rapidly rearranged to suit different missions. One day, the SRA-1 could carry up to 18 people, and the next it could be used as a freighter to carry 6,000 pounds of cargo, or even as a weapons platform. The GIII was modified to carry Harpoon antiship missiles, Sting Ray torpedoes or Paveway laser-guided bombs, as well as equipment to detect submarines.[22]

Foreign governments and international entities soon embraced the versatility of the GIII. Algeria, Egypt and Saudi Arabia were among its initial foreign customers, and early in 1983, the United Nations secretary-general, Javier Perez de Cuellar, took a nine-country tour on a Procter & Gamble GIII. The trip was a demonstration, however, and the United Nations did not buy an airplane.

Flying High

Meanwhile, signs pointing to an industry recovery were appearing, and Gulfstream continued to perform well. In the third quarter of 1983, 10 GIIIs and 10 Commander turboprops were delivered.

The SRA-1, the military version of the GIII, was a versatile aircraft. It could serve as a weapons platform, and its interior could be quickly configured to transport people or cargo, depending on the mission. *(Photo courtesy of Gulfstream Aerospace.)*

At Christmas, Gulfstream's employees pitched in to take out a full-page newspaper ad in the *Savannah News-Press* wishing Allen Paulson a Merry Christmas and thanking him for a good year.

And a good year it had been. Gulfstream Aerospace was the only aircraft manufacturer whose growth in revenue and earnings was uninterrupted through even the darkest days. Its earnings for 1983 had increased from $43 million to $51 million, on revenues of $586 million. The increase is even more impressive because revenue had gone up only slightly — just $3 million — between the end of 1982 and the end of 1983.

As 1984 began, rumors swirled that General Dynamics or some other cash-rich corporation was thinking of acquiring Gulfstream. Responding to the rumors, Allen Paulson enigmatically told a *Business Week* reporter that he "wouldn't preclude that possibility."[23]

It wouldn't be General Dynamics, however, or at least not yet. With a 3 percent stake in the Cessna Aircraft Company, the defense giant decided to purchase that aviation company in 1985. (See Chapter Nine.)

Unwanted Attention

As Gulfstream prospered, Allen Paulson began diversifying his interests. He bought nearly 25 percent of the outstanding stock of Wheeling-Pittsburgh Steel Corporation and indulged his love of horse racing by paying $800,000 for the brother of Croesco, winner of the Florida Derby. He also paid $1.6 million for 13 thoroughbreds in Kentucky and $5.4 million for 10 yearlings in Lexington, Virginia.[24]

Paulson also contributed generously to a number of causes and civic projects, such as Georgia Southern University, to which he gave $1 million to help build a football stadium. His con-

tribution was reported in the *Savannah Morning News* in late 1983.

Two men read about the contribution and started to toy with the idea of kidnapping Paulson's 28-year-old son, John Michael Paulson, and ransoming him for $1.2 million. What started out as idle talk degenerated into actual planning.

About two months later, the men, neither of whom worked at Gulfstream, went to the younger Paulson's home in Savannah and waited in the bushes for him to come home. They jumped John Paulson as he walked from his car to his front door. Wrestling him back to his car, they demanded his keys. Paulson reached for his double-cham-

Egypt was an early customer of the GIII. Egyptian President Hosni Mubarak (center) is shown here with a GIV crew and members of the Egyptian air force. Gulfstream pilot Bob Smyth is on Mubarak's left. *(Photo courtesy of Bob Smyth.)*

bered .22-caliber derringer pistol instead. He fired at both men, wounding one fatally. The other ran off but was captured a few hours later. He was eventually convicted and sent to prison.[25]

As a result, security was immediately tightened at Gulfstream Aerospace and new safety measures were implemented to discourage future attempts.

Closing the Commander Line

The turboprop line did not share in the company's overall prosperity. In 1982, the Bethany plant was forced to lay off workers and shut down production for 44 days. Many factors were working against the Commander (and the Peregrine, which was still under development). High interest rates and an influx of liability lawsuits that sent insurance premiums through the roof were two of the most pernicious reasons. In addition, the market for twin turboprops was saturated. Like many aviation companies, Gulfstream kept waiting for the turnaround, but losses in the Bethany operation continued to mount.

Finally, in January 1985, Gulfstream announced it was shutting down the Bethany plant, which had been producing Aero Commanders for more than 35 years, and suspending the development of the single-fanjet Peregrine aircraft. This wasn't the end for the Commander line, however; in 1988, new investors acquired the rights to the Commander 112 and 114, and production at the Bethany plant was revived. (The rights to the Aero Commander were eventually sold to a company in Washington state.)[26]

The reason the Commander suffered while the more expensive Gulfstreams continued to sell was simple — large corporations saw their long-range jets as business assets and not luxuries. Even during the worst recessions, corporate flying was too valuable to sacrifice. On the other hand, turboprops, purchased by small companies and private individuals, were seen as expendable luxuries.

But a study conducted by Aviation Data Services in 1983 noted a correlation between a company's financial performance and whether it owned a business aircraft. The study affirmed that *Fortune* 500 companies that operated one or more business aircraft did better financially than those without. "While no one can prove a cause-and-effect," commented *Dun's Business Month*, "it's a safe bet that their top managers out on the road aren't sitting around hub airports waiting for connecting flights."[27]

Gulfstream ended the development of the Peregrine military trainer in 1985. Pictured is a concept for a side-by-side version of the trainer. *(Image courtesy of Bob Cooper.)*

There was still the damaging perception, however, that corporate jets were opulent excesses of management. (During the federal bailout of Chrysler Corporation in 1979, for instance, the government told Chrysler to sell off its three Gulfstreams. Only after Chrysler became profitable again, in 1983, was it permitted to purchase another business jet — this time a GIII.)

The perception led to proposed legislation that briefly hurt sales of business jets before cooler heads prevailed. In the summer of 1984, the Internal Revenue Service proposed a "90 percent use test." An owner had to prove that an airplane was used for business purposes 90 percent of the time or lose all rights to deductions. The old rule called for a 50 percent test. The measure was eventually dropped.[28]

Later that year, President Ronald Reagan wanted to eliminate the Investment Tax Credit and lengthen the depreciation allowance from five years to 12 years. This measure, too, eventually dried up and died, but the threat of the tax credit's elimination remained. This threat contributed to the aviation industry's stagnation.

Joining the Ranks of the *Fortune* 500

The legislative battles did not have any lasting effects on Gulfstream Aerospace, however. Between November 6 and November 16, 1984, the company booked more than $80 million in new orders for the SRA-1 and the civilian GIII, as well as advance orders for the GIV. By March, Gulfstream, with a backlog of more than $800 million, had arrived on the *Fortune* 500 list, ranking No. 417, and just five months later its order backlog reached $1 billion. Gulfstream held 13 percent of the business jet market.

Analysts who followed Gulfstream's stock kept it in the "buy" column even during the industry's down years. "Gulfstream has the best products for the markets it serves," noted one analyst writing for *Business Week*.[29] Another, writing for *Dun's Business Month*, rated the GIII as "the most wanted corporate jet on the market despite its $14 million-plus price tag."

"Gulfstream Aerospace has long mystified business aircraft manufacturers, who have wracked their brains trying to figure out what GA is doing right, bucking seemingly implacable market trends and painting its books with great slathers of black ink."[30]

By the mid-1980s, Gulfstream Aerospace had become a truly international company with more than 60 percent of sales coming from overseas. International sales of the GI and GII, by contrast, had been 40 percent. Gulfstream's technical support and field service representatives were spread across the world to deliver support 24 hours a day, 365 days a year. These representatives maintained the tradition of dedication and resourcefulness that had characterized Gulfstream from the beginning.

Field Representative Tony Duncan, who was stationed in England at the time, recalled one of his most unusual experiences as a rep. He helped the operators of a GII who had made an emergency landing on a racetrack in Ireland. A special runway had to be constructed to get the aircraft off the racetrack.

"It takes a very dedicated, knowledgeable, tolerant individual to perform satisfactorily as a field service representative," noted Albert Glenn, who was appointed executive vice president in 1983.

"He must know when to talk, when to listen and above all, maintain a constant line of communication with the company. He is our link with those who purchase our products and their satisfaction with this product plays a very definite role in the future of every one of us."[31]

The Gulfstream IV was "evolutionary by design" and "revolutionary in concept." *(Photo courtesy of Gulfstream Aerospace.)*

CHAPTER EIGHT

THE GULFSTREAM IV:
A REVOLUTIONARY CONCEPT

"Writing about the GIV is both a joy and a frustration. There is not a more exciting airplane in corporate aviation, yet there is so much to experience and write about that one doesn't know where to stop. Gulfstream isn't stopping either.... Can the airplane get any better? It's hard to imagine how, but the Gulfstream has always been able to do it."

— Flying magazine, 1987[1]

THE TAY ENGINE WAS THE breakthrough needed to make the Gulfstream IV a success, but it took Charles Coppi months of patient badgering to get the rest of the company to realize it. The experience, he recalled years later, was "probably the closest I came to being fired in my career."[2]

In early 1982, Allen Paulson had all but settled on the idea of a four-engine airplane that would have used an engine called the RB401, a smaller, quieter and cleaner engine than the Spey.

The Spey was a strong engine and had powered both the GII and the GIII with an impressive record for reliability. But it had a number of drawbacks that precluded its use on another Gulfstream. It was noisy, emitted more air pollution than recent legislation allowed and was not as fuel efficient as the times called for. The oil crises and environmental movements of the last 15 years had left lasting marks on the aviation industry.

But whereas the Spey was rated at 11,400 pounds of thrust, the RB401 put out only 6,000. That meant four would have been required to give the GIV greater range and cruising speed, the two areas that still topped customers' wish lists.

The design work for a four-engine airplane had advanced far enough for Gulfstream to get assurance from the FAA that a four-engine configuration was within federal aviation regulations. Operators were even given a sneak preview at Gulfstream's annual operators' workshop in early 1982.

It wasn't the most desirable solution, however, because four engines meant an almost total redesign of the Gulfstream. Instead of shaping an evolutionary successor built upon previous (and proven) experience, engineers had to start almost from square one. "There's an old rule in airplane design," commented Coppi. "You only use the number of engines that will satisfy the mission.

"If it's two, it's two. If you don't have the right sizing for two, then you think about three and four. We figured we'd just hang four engines on the GIV and walk away from it. It would have been quiet and a little cleaner. But the effect spreads like a disease, affecting the airplane's structure, systems, engine control, everything."[3]

Another issue with the RB401 was that it would never accumulate valuable airline time. Engines on airliners accumulate more hours than those on business jets, which benefit from the air-

A model of the GIV with just two engines. The GIV built upon proven technology. *(Photo courtesy of Gulfstream Aerospace.)*

liners' experience. Any maintenance issues will be first seen on the airliners' engines, but the 401 was too small to ever be used on an airliner. In addition, a four-engine Gulfstream would face a tougher certification schedule by the FAA because the design was so different.

Nevertheless, Gulfstream and Rolls-Royce engineers were hard at work to make the 401 fit within the mission requirements of more than 4,000 nautical miles at a cruising speed of more than Mach .8. There was a perception among some at Gulfstream that four engines were better than two, and Paulson had bought into that view. Rolls-Royce was pushing the 401 because it wanted to develop the engine for both military and business applications.

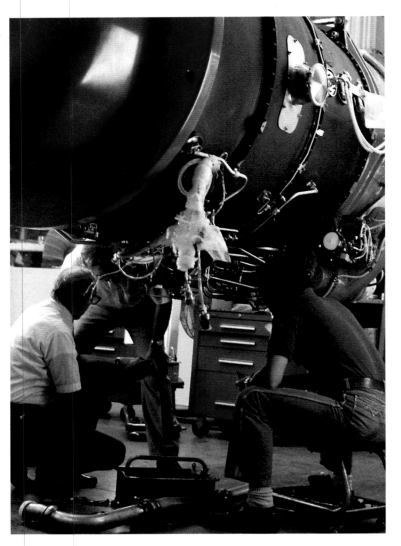

But in February 1982, Coppi received a phone call from chief engineer John Ashmole, a long-time friend at Rolls-Royce, who told him about the Tay. The Tay was being conceived for the proposed Fokker 100, a 100-seat commuter airliner. The engineers agreed that the Tay concept would solve most of the issues Gulfstream faced with the GIV. It would be able to perform the mission within the guidelines and restrictions imposed by the FAA, and do it with just two engines.

This was important information and almost cost Ashmole his job, recalled Norman Wilson, who worked for Ashmole. "We weren't supposed to talk about the Tay to anyone except Fokker," he said.[4]

Knowing he faced an uphill struggle, Coppi built his case carefully. A month later, he attended a meeting of Rolls-Royce and Gulfstream engineers held during the Heritage Golf Classic in Hilton Head, South Carolina. When the time was right, he broached the subject of the Tay.

"Wow, you would have thought the roof fell in. It got very quiet and very cold in that room. We had gotten pretty far downstream with the four-engine configuration, and now I was in the process of upsetting a lot of people's ideas, including those of Rolls-Royce, which had planned to develop and introduce this RB401. They had larger market considerations for that kind of engine."[5]

Coppi persisted, pointing out all the advantages the Tay offered over the 401. After the meeting, he took his argument back to Gulfstream, where he presented all the same arguments.

"You could just feel that we were derailing something. There was this mantra that 'four engines are better than two,' but we kept at it and stayed above the politics. I just put the technical arguments on the table — we wanted airline experience behind the engine, it would satisfy the market, it was easier to integrate, etc. We ordered

The Tay engine, being worked on by Rolls-Royce engineers. The Tay was the key to the design of the GIV and demonstrated the close relationship between Gulfstream and Rolls-Royce. *(Photo courtesy of Gulfstream Aerospace.)*

up a pretty large design review with Rolls-Royce. The Tay turned out to be the answer that really pulled the GIV together."[6]

Named for a river in Scotland, the Tay allowed engineers to meet all of the mission requirements while adhering to the FAA's regulations. As an added bonus, a unique three-way development team was established: Rolls, Gulfstream and Fokker. The collaboration saved both time and money.

A High-Altitude Balancing Act

Noise pollution in the vicinity of airports surfaced as a serious problem in the early 1960s. The combination of noisy first-generation turbojets, with low bypass ratios and slow climb performance, and the increasing numbers of airliners resulted in a public outcry that ultimately put many planned airport expansions on hold for a number of years. Many airports, such as National Airport (now Ronald Reagan National Airport) in Washington, D.C., responded with strict noise curfews.

One of the few drawbacks to the Spey engine was its high noise output, so the engine was modified with a "hush kit" developed by Rolls-Royce. A five-chute exhaust nozzle and sound absorbing material in the jet pipe were installed to reduce jet noise. However, this modification slightly reduced the engine's performance at higher altitudes.[7]

Several hush kit concepts were tested to dampen the high noise emitted by the Spey engines on the GII and GIII. One unusual design, shown here, was unsuccessful. A five-chute exhaust nozzle was adopted and worked well. *(Photo courtesy of Bob Smyth.)*

In looking at the basic design of the engine cycle, the fundamental parameters that drive noise — the exhaust, the speed of the jet of air coming out of the back end and the fact that the engine is turning so rapidly — are very difficult to overcome.[8]

A balance needed to be found between the noisy low-bypass engines found on the GII and GIII and the high-bypass engines, which were quiet but lagged behind in other areas such as performance at high altitudes.

The Tay solved this problem by taking the core of the Mark 555 Spey engine, which had many hours of use on regional airliners, and adding a state-of-the-art fan assembly that was based on an airline engine designated the RB211. The bypass ratio was increased from an unacceptably noisy ratio of less than 1:1 to 3:1, making the engine quiet enough to operate during nighttime at National Airport.[9] Gulfstream wasn't content with just meeting the minimum federal standards; the company wanted to make sure that the customer had an airplane quiet enough so that its noise would never come up as an operational restriction.[10]

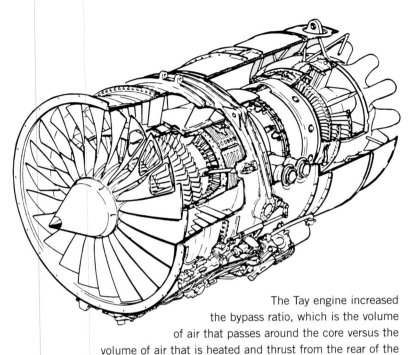

The Tay engine increased the bypass ratio, which is the volume of air that passes around the core versus the volume of air that is heated and thrust from the rear of the engine. *(Photo courtesy of Gulfstream Aerospace.)*

The fan section comprised a 44-inch-diameter fan with 22 wide-chord titanium blades. The intrinsically stiff blades were important for the engine's efficiency because two-thirds of the cruise thrust came from the fan.[11]

In the Gulfstream tradition of providing enough thrust to power an airliner, the Tay engine had 13,850 pounds of thrust. "The Tay kept the fuel efficiency and the power of the engine needed for high-altitude, high-speed flight, which was balanced against the ability of the engine to be designed for low noise and low smoke and pollutants," Coppi said.[12]

The Pieces Come Together

Coppi wrote in an article that the GIV was "evolutionary by design, revolutionary in concept." The GIV addressed all the shortcomings of the previous Gulfstream. Besides the environmental issues, the GIII occasionally struggled against high winds when it flew westbound over the Atlantic Ocean, so a way had to be found to increase the range beyond 3,600 nautical miles without adding too much weight.

A third factor was competition. Both Canadair and Falcon Jet were developing potential competitive alternatives to the GIII. The times were signaling for something new.

Responding to customer surveys, engineers aimed at reaching at least 4,000 nautical miles. They also increased the cruising speed because more time in the air could be fatiguing for the crew. The size of the cabin and the galley was increased as well, and with a 4.5-foot stretch, a sixth window was added.[13]

The GIV wing was designed to be 870 pounds lighter than the wing on the GIII. The new wing was much more aerodynamic and capable of holding 1,000 gallons more fuel. It retained the winglets, but maintenance access was improved by providing fewer and larger inspection covers on the lower wing surface. This change also cleaned up wing aerodynamics. In addition, wing leading-edge bleed air anti-icing protection was modified to a simplified, lighter-weight single-wall system.[14]

Flight International magazine noted that the aerodynamic changes made to the wing were almost imperceptible to the naked eye, but the improvements reduced wing drag by 5 percent.[15]

Overall, the performance efficiency of the GIV was 19 percent better than the GIII's.

Going Digital

It was inside the cockpit that an observer found the "most exotic and exciting aspect of the GIV," according to *Flying* magazine.

"Its six large Sperry [cathode ray] tubes display everything from primary flight instrumentation to the level of hydraulic fluid. All primary flight instruments — the basic T arrangement of attitude, airspeed, altitude, vertical speed and heading — appear on a single 8-by-8-inch tube in front of each pilot. A tube of identical size directly to the right displays all manner of navigation data, ranging from a big, old fashioned HSI [horizontal situation indicator] picture — called the Texas grapefruit display because of its size — to a course map of the flight plan stretching for more than 1,000 miles, including nav aids with identifiers."[16]

Gulfstream was one of the first civilian aviation companies to install digital flight management computers on aircraft. Paulson had ordered $100 million worth of the advanced electronics from Sperry Aerospace Group in 1985. (Sperry was acquired by Honeywell a year later.) Such deals usually took between nine and 18 months. In typical Paulson fashion, he negotiated terms in under three months.[17]

It was only a matter of time before such technology would find its way into aircraft, but that didn't make the transition any easier. In fact, when the first GIV was undergoing flight tests, the Sperry/Honeywell systems were installed on the right side of the cockpit and traditional "steam" gauges were installed on the left as a backup. Engineers didn't want to risk holding up testing should the new technology fail.

Gulfstream was a pioneer in the installation of digital equipment in the cockpit. The technology was revolutionary, and certifying the instruments was very difficult. *(Photo courtesy of Gulfstream Aerospace.)*

Developing and certifying flight software was perhaps the biggest challenge. "We were babes in the woods," noted Ted Mendenhall, one of the GIV's test pilots. "Some certification work had been done in the past, but the entire integrated system was new for us."[18]

False alarms were common. "For instance, hydraulic pressure may dip momentarily when you're activating a control," explained Mendenhall. "Well, you don't necessarily need a message to tell you that. A delay would keep you from seeing the message unless it was a real problem."[19]

Certifying a digital integrated flight system was new for the FAA as well. "That got us all educated in the arena of V and V — software verification and validation — which was a whole new discipline to the industry," noted Gulfstream engineer Ed Flinn. "We had a very difficult time with it."[20]

The rewards were well worth the effort because fuel efficiency increased and pilot workload dipped, making the airplane more comfortable and safer.

The first GIV was rolled out on September 11, 1985, ahead of schedule. Allen Paulson wanted to fly it to the 1985 NBAA Conference being held in New Orleans, so employees worked almost around the clock to get it ready. *(Photo courtesy of Gulfstream Aerospace.)*

Inset: Posing in front of the new GIV, from left to right, Albert Glenn, Allen Paulson and Bob Buckley.

Aerospace

The Debut of the GIV

Employees worked at a fever pitch to get the first GIV ready for flight in early September 1985 so it could be flown to the annual NBAA convention, held later that month in New Orleans. Paulson desperately wanted to make sure a gleaming GIV was on hand to steal the thunder from the three-engine Dassault Falcon 900, which was also to debut at the show.[21]

Odd shifts and around-the-clock work took place at the Savannah facility as the GIV went into final assembly. It was estimated that more than 700 employees, from management to production, were actively working on the Gulfstream IV, logging tens of thousands of hours to prepare for the September rollout.[22] "Goldie Glenn's people worked like hell," recalled Coppi. "When you have a labor of love, what drives you is to see this thing come together. It's no longer just lines on paper or diagrams on a computer screen."[23]

But as the deadline approached, it became clear that Rolls-Royce would not be finished with the Tay's testing program. Paulson wanted to speed up the pace, but Rolls insisted on staying on its original testing schedule. The company did agree, however, to clear two ground test engines to allow the GIV to take its initial flight tests and fly to the NBAA convention. The engines were housed in temporary glass fiber nacelles. "They were perfectly good engines," explained Bob Smyth, who flew in the chase plane for the GIV's initial flights. "They just had not reached the maturity that Rolls-Royce wanted."[24]

On September 19, 1985, three months ahead of schedule, the first prototype (N404GA) flew for the first time, piloted by Mendenhall and Lee Johnson. Five days later, Paulson himself flew the GIV to New Orleans, with Mendenhall and Johnson as his passengers. Workers called it the "GIII and a half" because the aircraft was still unfinished. The interior, for instance, was almost bare, and for that reason few people got to peek inside.

Aviation International News noted that "Gulfstream Aerospace defied all the predictions of the pundits and came here with its mighty

The actual GIV that flew to New Orleans was only half-finished. Few customers got to look inside. Instead, a mockup, shown below, was completed and shipped to the show, giving customers an idea of the GIV's plush interior. *(Photo courtesy of Gulfstream Aerospace.)*

The competition is still trying to catch up with this airplane.

For several years now, other aircraft manufacturers have been trying to design and build airplanes that could run in the same league with our Gulfstream III.

And we understand their motivation.

The Gulfstream III has been the overwhelming choice of a high-performance, long-range executive jet in the most demanding, sophisticated and prestigious arena in the business aircraft market. As a result, more than 165 Gulfstream IIIs are at work today with the world's major corporations and governments, flying their key executives and officials into every corner of the globe.

We've all seen concepts of what others think it takes to overtake the Gulfstream III.

One was a wider cabin. Another was three engines. But as good as the airplanes are that came from those ideas, they couldn't catch up with the Gulfstream III. Maybe that's why they never caught on as alternatives to it.

The most recent competitive concept promises something for everyone: a wider *and* higher cabin, three engines, *and* a hundred more miles of range.

And as good an airplane as it may turn out to be, evaluate it carefully and you find it's still just about where the Gulfstream III started.

Its cabin isn't as long, so an inch or two more in circumference hasn't made it more spacious than the cabin of the Gulfstream III.

Its three engines sound like a comforting idea, but even the airlines decided two are enough for a modern airplane. And the Gulfstream III has two of the most reliable turbofan engines ever put on an executive jet.

Its range advantage over the Gulfstream III, which looks good on paper, turns out to be fifteen minutes more in the air. That's not exactly what Gulfstream III pilots would call a quantum leap in their flight planning opportunities.

So as hard as they've been trying, it seems to us our competitors haven't yet caught on to what it takes to build an airplane that's going to catch up with our Gulfstream III, much less go beyond it.

But we know.

It takes a concept so advanced, it's revolutionary.

There is no way they can catch up with this one.

One thing we've learned in twenty-five years of designing and building airplanes is that it's always better to set the pace and let others try to catch up.

Consequently, we've spent our time developing business aircraft that not only fill specific needs, but set the standards for superiority in doing it.

That's how the Gulfstream I came about. And the Gulfstream II. And the Gulfstream III.

And now there's the Gulfstream IV.

We made sure this amazing airplane satisfies every demand the most professional business aircraft operators are going to put on their airplanes for the balance of this century.

They want the range to not only create totally new city-pair combinations, but to utilize the most efficient and prudent routes for long intercontinental flights. Only the Gulfstream IV lets them do it.

They need the speed to make a 5,000 statute mile flight non-stop in about 9 hours. Only the Gulfstream IV can do it.

Along with range and speed, it's imperative they have a cabin with the size and environment that encourages utilization of the airplane to its maximum. Only the Gulfstream IV provides it.

They want aircraft systems and flight management technology more advanced than those in commercial airliners.

Only the Gulfstream IV gives it to them.

They want an airplane that is as fuel-efficient and quiet as a flying machine can be. The Gulfstream IV is all of those things, too.

It wasn't easy getting to the Gulfstream IV.

It took a new wing. New engines. New computerized flight information systems. New technology in structures. New components. Even new techniques in the way we build airplanes.

But we got there. With a concept so advanced, it's revolutionary.

Along the way, we've also earned firm orders for more than 85 Gulfstream IVs, which we believe is the biggest backlog ever enjoyed by a new executive jet aircraft.

Now, others may tell you their airplanes are competing with the Gulfstream IV.

The truth is, it's alone on the track.

The ultimate in business aircraft will always be a Gulfstream.

We are in a unique position to work with you to develop an attractive financing plan for the purchase of a new Gulfstream III or to construct a lease arrangement with extremely favorable terms. To discuss a proposal, call or write Gulfstream Marketing, Gulfstream Aerospace Corporation. P.O. Box 2206, Savannah, Georgia 31402 U.S.A. Telephone: (912) 964-3274. Telex: 804705.

Gulfstream IV, landing with all of eight hours in its flight log."[25]

Paulson was joined in New Orleans by Lee Iacocca, the legendary savior of Chrysler Corporation. Iacocca was not at the show as a prospective customer, though he flew in a GIII. He was there as Paulson's boss because Chrysler had just completed the purchase of Gulfstream Aerospace a month earlier. (See Chapter Nine.)

The GIV was a hit even before the airplane flew. More than 80 orders were taken while the aircraft was under development. The backlog of almost $1.3 billion in orders was the biggest for a single aircraft in business aviation history.

The GIV received its Type Certification from the FAA in April 1987 and immediately set off to shatter world speed and distance records. Its capabilities were remarkable, exceeding many estimates by Gulfstream's own engineers.

With a maximum takeoff weight of 73,200 pounds, the GIV had a top speed of Mach .88 and a maximum altitude of 45,000 feet. Gulfstream

Even before the GIV took to the air for its first flight, Gulfstream had secured more than 80 orders. This ad highlights the fact that Gulfstream had no real competition. *(Image courtesy of Gulfstream Aerospace.)*

had originally planned to certify the airplane's maximum speed and altitude at Mach .85 and 45,000 feet, and engineers had targeted 4,000 nautical miles as the aircraft's IFR range. At its cruising speed of Mach .8, however, the GIV was certified for 4,300 nautical miles.

As *Flying* magazine noted:

"Writing about the GIV is both a joy and a frustration. There is not a more exciting airplane in corporate aviation, yet there is so much to experience and write about that one doesn't know where to stop. Gulfstream isn't stopping either.... Can the airplane get any better? It's hard to imagine how, but the Gulfstream has always been able to do it."[26]

In 1988, (left to right) John Salamankas, Allen Paulson, Bob Smyth and Jeff Bailey set a speed record flying eastbound in a GIV. *(Photo courtesy of Bob Smyth.)*

CHAPTER NINE

THE CHRYSLER YEARS

1985–1990

"We at Chrysler don't know much about building airplanes, but I like to think we know something about running companies. We bought Gulfstream because of its leadership, knowledge and its people."

— Lee Iacocca, 1985[1]

STANDING NEXT TO ALLEN Paulson at the 1985 NBAA conference, held that year in New Orleans, Lee Iacocca told the assembled media that he wished people would stop referring to the Gulfstream — now owned by Chrysler Corporation — as the "Cadillac of the industry. Rolls-Royce, maybe, but not Cadillac, pleeaasse."[2]

At the September conference, Iacocca exuded enthusiasm. He had turned around a virtually bankrupt corporation and made it into one on the prowl for acquisitions. Chrysler had completed the purchase of Gulfstream Aerospace in August, paying $637 million, half in cash and half in stock, barely denting the automaker's $3 billion in cash and securities.

Chrysler's acquisition followed the general strategy of the Big Three, which was to diversify away from the cyclical tendencies of the automotive market and move into high-tech industries. Two weeks prior to Chrysler's purchase of Gulfstream, General Motors had agreed to buy Hughes Aircraft for $5 billion, outbidding both Ford and Chrysler.

Though it was a minuscule part of Chrysler Corporation, Gulfstream had impressive earnings and revenues. The year it was purchased, Gulfstream recorded about $43 million in earnings on $602 million in revenue. Analysts noted that, by itself, Gulfstream would neither greatly help nor partic-

ularly hurt the giant automaker. As part of a larger diversification strategy, however, it could help even out the peaks and valleys in the automotive market.

The Gulfstream purchase was just the latest in a wave of acquisitions sweeping the still-troubled aviation industry. In addition to General Motors' huge acquisition of Hughes Aircraft, General Dynamics bought Cessna, Raytheon purchased Beech, Lear Siegler took over Piper Aircraft, and Bombardier purchased Canadair, maker of the Challenger.

Iacocca's decision to buy Gulfstream was sharply scrutinized by industry analysts. Many asserted that he did it for the prestige of owning Gulfstream, and that as long as Chrysler owned Gulfstream, Iacocca would fly in the most lavishly outfitted executive jet in the industry. It was true that Iacocca had long been a fan of Gulfstream (Chrysler owned two when it purchased Gulfstream Aerospace), but then so was anyone who could afford the aircraft. He dismissed that rationale during the NBAA show.

A resurgent Chrysler Corporation sought to diversify from the cyclical nature of the automobile industry by buying Gulfstream Aerospace.

Lee Iacocca (left) and Allen Paulson held a press conference at
the New Orleans Convention Center, where the GIV was unveiled.
Iacocca asked the press not to refer to the aircraft as the "Cadillac
of the industry." *(Photo courtesy of Gulfstream Aerospace.)*

"I'm not going to go on TV like the guy who sells
the razors [Remington chief Victor Kiam]," Iacocca
told the press.

*"We at Chrysler don't know much about building
airplanes, but I like to think we know something
about running companies. We bought Gulfstream
because of its leadership, knowledge and its people."[3]*

He explained that there were two reasons
behind the purchase: diversification opportunities
and "technical synergism," or in plain language,
technology transfer between the two companies.
How much Chrysler stood to benefit from Gulfstream
(and vice versa) from a technological perspective was
not clear, however. Chrysler news releases briefly
mentioned that some benefit could be derived from

Gulfstream's work with lighter and stronger com-
posite material, as well as its experience with state-
of-the-art electronics. Paulson further suggested
that Chrysler might be interested in Gulfstream's
braking system, which had been adapted from what
was used on the F-16 fighter.

But on the whole, analysts accepted only the
first reason — diversification — as the logical rationale behind the acquisition. After he announced the
acquisition of Gulfstream, Iacocca noted that
Chrysler was prepared to make other large diversification moves in the areas of high technology. He
also promised not to interfere with the way Gulfstream
Aerospace ran itself.

Initially, Iacocca was true to his word — Paulson
and his management team remained in control
of Gulfstream, and Paulson agreed to stay on for
five years.

"A lot of people get something going, make some
money, and then pull out," Paulson said in a 1999
interview. "I never did that. I just let it all ride. But
there came a period when I figured it was a good
opportunity to sell and still be involved in Gulfstream.
So I sold it."[4]

Paulson may have had another reason to want
to sell. One of his interests, Wheeling-Pittsburgh
Steel Corporation, had filed for bankruptcy protection. The *Wall Street Journal* reported that Paulson
had about $50.5 million invested in 34 percent of
the steelmaker's shares.

*"Allen Paulson's personal financial problems
may be behind his decision to sell.... It would be a
remarkable divestiture for the hands-on manager
of this maker of corporate jets, an erstwhile auto
mechanic who still makes two or three daily circuits
of its sprawling assembly plant in Savannah."[5]*

Whatever the reason behind Paulson's decision
to sell and Iacocca's decision to buy, Gulfstreamers
were enthusiastic, even relieved, because they now
had the backing of a large, well-capitalized parent.
"Everybody thought this was great," recalled Albert
Glenn. "We figured more money would be available
to develop new aircraft."[6]

There were perks that came with being an
executive in a Big Three automaker. Each year,
executives were allowed to "test drive" three brand-
new Chrysler cars for free. After four months, the

driver wrote a paragraph describing his or her experience with the vehicle, then turned the car in for a new model to drive for four more months. Even the gas was free.

"You could get a Jeep Cherokee, a Jeep Wrangler or a Chrysler New Yorker," Bob Smyth fondly recalled. "Whatever they had then. Everything was available, and you could lease cars for your family under very favorable conditions on a yearly basis. They didn't get free gas, though."[7]

In his official announcement, Iacocca warmly welcomed Gulfstream into the family of Chrysler Corporation. But not everyone in the parent organization was happy with Chrysler's movements outside the automotive industry. Hal Sperlich, a member of Iacocca's office of the chief executive, was particularly upset. Sperlich was a committed car man who loved nothing more than to watch new automotive ideas evolve from paper to metal.

In Sperlich's mind, the $3 billion Chrysler had in its treasury was better spent on new car designs than on nonautomotive acquisitions.

Iacocca disagreed, and he rejected Sperlich's many requests for more money for automotive research. In fact, less than a year after Gulfstream was acquired, Iacocca turned Chrysler Corporation into a holding company with four businesses: Chrysler Motors, Chrysler Financial, Chrysler Technologies and Gulfstream Aerospace.

On the Production Line

On the shop floor of Gulfstream, very little changed. Jerry Greenwald, Iacocca's right-hand man at Chrysler, took a tour shortly after the purchase, asking questions to see if the subsidiary's production could be improved. "He asked me 'How long does it take you to build an airplane,' " recalled Bill Bauer, then director of manufacturing technologies.

"At the time we were building about three a month, so, on average, we built an airplane every seven days. He said, 'Seven days!?! We build a car every 20 seconds.' But we can't build an airplane like that because we work on a different curve."[8]

Very little changed when Chrysler bought Gulfstream. A Chrysler senior vice president looked for ways to improve production through automation, but the volume didn't justify the expense. *(Photo courtesy of Gulfstream Aerospace.)*

Bauer said they looked into automation, like that on the Chrysler line, but volume just didn't justify the cost of the equipment.

Perhaps the biggest potential change came when union organizers tried to unionize Gulfstream's workforce. Gulfstream had been union-free at Savannah since the plant was founded. But almost immediately after the acquisition, the United Auto, Aerospace and Agriculture Workers union began to collect signature cards from Gulfstream employees. Signature cards had to be obtained from a third of the Gulfstream workers for the National Labor Relations Board to call for a vote on whether to allow the union to represent workers.

In August 1986, after gathering signatures for a year, the union filed a petition with the NLRB to permit a vote, and the board held a hearing to determine what job positions could be included in the category of maintenance and production workers, which the union was seeking to represent.[9] But the union abandoned its effort just two months later. Though almost 2,500 of the roughly 3,000 workers at Gulfstream were eligible to vote, it was clear even before a vote that workers did not desire a union. Allen Paulson issued a statement about the failed unionizing attempt:

"The union, in abandoning its supporters and the elections, seems to have learned what we have known all along — the people of Gulfstream have been an independent workforce since the Gulfstream plant was established here 19 years ago.... By their lack of enthusiasm for any union organizing attempt they certainly indicated their preference to remain independent and free of outside interference. We are very proud of them."[10]

The shop has remained union-free through the years. "We've got a nice plan," explained long-time Gulfstreamer Knoxie Crocker. "We just don't need a union."[11]

Crocker, who celebrated 34 years as part of Gulfstream in 1999, typifies the workforce, whose pride has been built into every Gulfstream from the beginning. When she was interviewed in 1999, Crocker sported gold GIV earrings and her 15-year, 20-year and 25-year pins. "I'm trying to figure out what I'm going to do with my 30-year pin," she said.[12]

The changes in Gulfstream's ownership did not affect the quality of the work. New hires still went through the same rigorous orientation to ensure that quality remained the highest priority. "When they get their job training, we really stress to do it right the first time," Crocker explained.

"If you make a mistake, well, nobody's perfect. Just don't try to hide it. We ain't gonna shoot you if you mess up something, but we're liable to shoot you if you don't tell us about it. Quality is what put us where we are today, number one in the industry."[13]

Employees were rapidly added during this period. In March 1986, the company expanded its completion operations to the West Coast with Chrysler's purchase of AiResearch Aviation, located in Long Beach, California. As part of the deal, more than 100 AiResearch technicians, managers and administrative personnel were hired. The intent was to use the facility not only for completions but as a major service center for aircraft based in the West.[14]

By 1987, the company's employment figures had risen to about 4,000 and were predicted to continue climbing by 15 percent to 20 percent over the next year to ramp up for production of the GIV.[15]

With Chrysler's blessing, Allen Paulson's role at Gulfstream changed. He relinquished the presidency in 1986 to Albert Glenn. "They felt that Allen should be a little more outside the company, looking for acquisitions and such," Glenn said. "So I was made president. I was 'Mr. Inside' and Allen was 'Mr. Outside.'"[16]

'Round the World, Again and Again

Being "Mr. Outside" gave Paulson the chance to personally set and shatter more world records. The GIV had been certified on April 22, 1987 (on Paulson's birthday), and two months later he girdled the globe in the airplane, flying westbound against the wind currents. Even with the wind against him, Paulson managed to set 24 speed records during the flight.

Four others accompanied him: John Salamankas, Keith Carter Edgecomb, Jefferson

Above: After the acquisition by Chrysler, Allen Paulson became less involved in the day-to-day activities of Gulfstream. Instead, he became part cheerleader and part strategist. *(Photo courtesy of Gulfstream Aerospace.)*

Left: In 1986, Gulfstream's completions capacity was boosted with the acquisition of AiResearch Aviation in Long Beach, California. The center was soon used as a major service center in the West. *(Photo courtesy of Gulfstream Aerospace.)*

Bailey and Colin Brady Allen. The five men began their 19,843-nautical-mile odyssey at Le Bourget Airport, near Paris, where Charles Lindbergh ended his historical flight 60 years earlier.[17] *Aviation International News* covered the 36-hour, eight-minute flight.

The *Pursuit of Perfection* is the airplane in which John Salamankas, Allen Paulson, Bob Smyth and Jeff Bailey set 11 world speed records for flying around the globe eastbound in 1988. The GIV circumnavigated the world in just 36 hours, eight minutes and 24 seconds, beating the previous record, set by a 747, by 45 minutes. *(Photo courtesy of Bob Smyth.)*

"Gulfstream Aerospace's round-the-world Gulfstream IV broke out of the clouds and mists before a cheering crowd early Sunday afternoon at Le Bourget Airport, made an intentionally long low approach to fly past the spectator-laden line of chalets, then gracefully touched down on Runway 3-21 with some 20 world records in tow, including an east-to-west global circuit."[18]

The record breaking continued. In 1988, Paulson was at it again when he set another world speed record, this time going eastbound. Paulson's GIV, named *Pursuit of Perfection*, touched down in Houston at 9:27 p.m., completing the easterly circumnavigation of the world in 36 hours, 8 minutes and 24 seconds. By a little more than 45 minutes, the GIV had broken the record set less than a month earlier by a Boeing 747.[19]

A total of 11 around-the-world records were set during the trip, including records in both the National Aeronautical Association's Unlimited category and in the C-1.k class 55,000-pound-to-77,000-pound category.[20] The aircraft, which had been stripped, at the beginning of the trip had just 10 hours of flight time on the airframe and was equipped with an extra internal 1,200-gallon fuel tank.[21]

Paulson and Gulfstream were winning a slew of awards. In 1985, Paulson had won the Horatio Alger

Award. This award is given annually by the Horatio Alger Association of Distinguished Americans to people who exemplify the merits of the free enterprise system by triumphing over adverse circumstances. He was in good company — previous winners included presidents Reagan, Ford, Eisenhower and Hoover.[22]

Then in 1986 he became the 40th recipient of the Wright Brothers Memorial Trophy, joining the ranks of Charles Lindbergh and James Doolittle. The award is one of the most prestigious in the aviation industry, which debuted in 1948 to commemorate the Wright brothers' flight on December

Left: Paulson was awarded the prestigious Wright Brothers Memorial Trophy in 1986 for "significant public service of enduring value to aviation in the United States." *(Photo courtesy of Gulfstream Aerospace.)*

Left: An artist's conception of the supersonic business jet. *(Image courtesy of Gulfstream Aerospace.)*

Below: Gulfstream and the Russian aircraft manufacturer Sukhoi cooperated on the initial design of the supersonic business jet. This 1989 photo shows Allen Paulson and Charles Coppi conferring with their Soviet counterparts on the design. The woman at the head of the table is the interpreter, Paulson is to her left and next to him is Coppi. Bob Smyth is standing behind Paulson. To the interpreter's right is Mikhail Simonov, Sukhoi's chief designer. *(Photo courtesy of Bob Smyth.)*

17, 1903.[23] The trophy committee said that Paulson was chosen because he had been "instrumental in promoting general growth and heightening public interest in aviation affairs. His companies through the years have developed a variety of leading-edge technology aircraft to suit both civil and government needs and he has been a promoter of general aviation safety."

This particular award flew in the face of many analysts who dismissed the idea that Gulfstream aircraft were platforms for new technology. Some scoffed at Iacocca's assertion that Chrysler's acquisition was a foray into the area of high technology. One even said that "Gulfstream doesn't have any technology. It's just very good at putting chandeliers in luxury jets and charging corporations a lot of money for them."[24]

What this analyst failed to grasp was that the avionics in the GIV were soon incorporated as standard equipment in the aviation industry. For instance, Gulfstream was one of the first aviation companies to embrace the Global Positioning System along with state-of-the-art airborne weather radar, capable of detecting turbulence, and a lightning detector, which could sense the range and bearing of a lightning strike. Gulfstream also began installing custom-designed satellite communications equipment for telephone and data transmissions to turn the GIV into an "office-in-the-sky."[25]

In 1988, Paulson was again recognized for his contributions to aviation when he received the 10th annual Horward R. Hughes Award, joining recipients that included Chuck Yeager, the first man to fly faster than the speed of sound, aviation pioneer John K. Northrop and astronaut Charles "Peter" Conrad.

That year Gulfstream began developing a supersonic jet program. *Popular Mechanics* noted that the company was outlining requirements for a supersonic corporate jet, to be available by 2000. The 100-foot-long plane reportedly would have "a deeply swept delta-wing formation with twin-canted vertical stabilizers and forward canards. Wingspan would be 60 feet. It would carry 10 to 12 passengers and a crew of two. The primary obstacle remains the elimination of sonic booms while flying over land."[26]

According to a statement made by Allen Paulson, the corporate jet grew from a research study of Gulfstream aircraft owners and operators.[27]

With the end of the Cold War in 1989, Gulfstream teamed up with the Soviet Sukhoi Design Bureau to jointly develop a supersonic business jet. Paulson inked the deal for the proposed aircraft during a trip to the USSR. Under the agreement, Sukhoi was to design and build the airframe and landing gear, and Gulfstream was to be responsible for systems integration.

The Edge of the Edge

But clouds were once again gathering on the horizon, and this time Gulfstream Aerospace would not escape the turbulence. The GIV's unprecedented $1.5 billion backlog was being whittled down as the pace of new orders slowed because of the number of high-quality used aircraft available. In a way, Gulfstream was becoming a victim of its own success. One article noted that perhaps these jets were built "too well."

By 1989, production had returned to normal, which meant customers waited one year, instead of three, for their orders. Gulfstream, meanwhile, was reorganized with another Chrysler acquisition — Electrospace Systems — under Chrysler Technologies, of which Glenn was named vice chairman. John Sandford became president of Gulfstream.

Paulson's time wasn't all spent sitting in the cockpit of a GIV. He sought acquisitions and joint ventures to continue to grow Gulfstream Aerospace. Along with its partnership with Sukhoi to design a supersonic jet, Gulfstream had teamed up with Ed Swearingen, the veteran airplane designer who helped design the Fairchild Metro and Lockheed JetStar II, to design the Gulfjet, a smaller, entry-level business jet.

The partnership was dissolved in September 1989 because Paulson was concentrating on acquiring Learjet, based in Wichita, Kansas. Speculation swirled in the press about a possible merger because Paulson's GIV was often seen landing in Wichita.

But Chrysler was heading toward hard times once again. Foreign competition was beginning to cut into the Big Three's sales. After its near-death

The idea of a supersonic business jet (SBJ) grew from a research study conducted by Gulfstream which asked customers what ideas they had for business travel in the 21st century. The idea would eventually be shelved in the early 1990s, but the concept would again emerge in 1999. Although costly, an SBJ is technically feasible. *(Photo courtesy of Gulfstream Aerospace.)*

experience earlier in the decade, Chrysler lost no time in battening down the hatches. Jerry Greenwald went so far as to say that "This could be a fight to the death."[28] Chrysler's brush with bankruptcy had clearly left its mark; it was the most pessimistic of the Big Three, predicting a drop in auto sales as much as 4 percent the following year. The automaker's position was by no means on the brink, but pundits repeatedly quipped that Chrysler was "on the brink of the brink."

As a consequence, a battle had broken out among Chrysler's senior executives over the fate of its nonautomotive subsidiaries. The automotive faction, led by Hal Sperlich, won. In their view, the money Chrysler was committing to Gulfstream's research and development was better spent on developing a new base car with which it could beat back surging Japanese imports.

Meanwhile, no one at Gulfstream was aware that a decision had been made on Gulfstream's fate. In September 1989, a proposal was made in New York to Chrysler's finance committee to buy Lear. Glenn headed up a due diligence team at Lear but was not invited to the finance committee meetings. The committee approved the plan, and Paulson prepared for a meeting of the whole board the following day, and Glenn flew back to Savannah to await the decision.

The next morning, Paulson entered the board room to finalize the details. He didn't talk to Glenn again until well after lunchtime.

"I said, 'What the hell happened?'" Glenn recalled. "He said Iacocca told him, 'Paulson, we're not going to buy Lear. We're going to sell Gulfstream.' Just like that. The automobile faction had won."[29]

When the announcement was made public in December, Iacocca insisted that diversification itself hadn't been a mistake, but that buying and managing these companies didn't allow executives to concentrate on the business of making and selling cars.

Paulson took a leave of absence immediately after Chrysler's intention was made public in December. He intended to buy the company back and according to SEC regulations had to distance himself from Chrysler Technologies to be an eligible buyer. (Sandford, meanwhile, had taken another executive position with Chrysler Technologies outside Gulfstream. He eventually went to Rolls-Royce.) Albert "Goldie" Glenn once again became president as well as acting chairman during this interim period.

Iacocca had intended to auction off Gulfstream to the highest bidder. More than a dozen groups showed immediate interest. One of these groups was headed by Ted Forstmann. Forstmann, however, had no intention of getting into a bidding war.

"Master of the LBO"

When he heard that Gulfstream was for sale, Forstmann, then a founding partner of Forstmann Little & Company, was immediately interested. As described by author Daniel Kadlec in the insightful *Masters of the Universe*, Forstmann had been a satisfied customer of Gulfstream for years. The jet allowed him to "work and rest in leathery comfort while jetting from one company to another, from one investment partner to another, and from one philanthropic event to another anywhere in the world," wrote Kadlec.

"Here was the perfect company, [Forstmann] thought. It dominated its business, had a great product and was being let go by a giant company that simply didn't have the time or resources to devote to it because its main business was cars — not jets."[30]

Kadlec described Forstmann as the master of the leveraged buyout ("LBO" in the Wall Street lexicon). Forstmann founded Forstmann Little & Company with his brother, Nick, and William Brian Little, an investment banker, in 1978.

According to a *Business Week* profile, each shared in all aspects of running the firm but the three men had their own specialties: Little was the strategist, Nick was the number-cruncher, and Ted was the man who could raise capital. From 1978 to 1990, Forstmann Little & Company had engineered 14 LBOs worth more than $7 billion, including Dr Pepper (bought in 1984 for $650 million; sold in pieces for a total of $878 million two years later) and Topps. Forstmann had taken Topps private for $98 million and within two years reaped $204 million through two public offerings while retaining control of 55 percent of the stock.[31]

Forstmann had taken a respite from LBO deals in 1987 because junk-bond financing had pushed prices for companies too high. By 1990, however, junk bonds were in the doghouse as a financing vehicle, and Forstmann was ready to enter the game again. He managed to set up an interview with Allen Paulson at Paulson's Palm Springs, California, estate.

During the meeting, Paulson told Forstmann that Gulfstream had been hampered by Chrysler's way of doing things, which added unnecessary time and cost. In fact, he would later tell *Aviation Week & Space Technology* that Chrysler's requirements for reports, meetings and travel added as much as $20 million to $30 million a year to Gulfstream's overhead. "I felt I became less productive than I was capable of being, with all the controls," he told the magazine. "It was a different culture."[32]

Paulson was still looking into acquiring Learjet. "I figured if I can't buy Gulfstream back, I'd go ahead and buy Learjet and have something to play with," he explained in 1999.[33] As it turned out, he and Forstmann quickly came to an agreement to buy both companies, with Paulson investing $15 million of his own money. His stake and the fact that he would stay on to run Gulfstream Aerospace, plus extensive due diligence, laid the groundwork for the acquisition.

The deal to buy Learjet for $60 million fell through because its parent company, Integrated Resources, filed for Chapter 11 bankruptcy protection. Gulfstream's chief rival, Bombardier, eventually purchased the struggling company for $75 million.

Forstmann, Paulson and Iacocca got together and hammered out a deal before the formal bidding could take place. For $850 million, Gulfstream Aerospace was once again a private company with Paulson as chairman and CEO. He owned 32 percent and Forstmann Little owned 68 percent.

On March 30, a new board of directors was appointed with Allen Paulson remaining as chairman and CEO. The directors included Ted Forstmann, his brother Nicholas Forstmann and Brian Little, all general partners in Forstmann

Little & Company; William Acquavella, chairman of Acquavella Art Galleries; Robert Anderson, chairman emeritus of Rockwell International; Vicomte Etienne Davignon, executive director of Societe Generale de Belgique; Daniel Gill, chairman of Bausch & Lomb; Drew Lewis, chairman of Union Pacific Corporation and former secretary of transportation for President Ronald Reagan; Lt. Gen. Thomas Stafford, United States Air Force, a former command pilot for the Gemini and Apollo space missions; Robert Strauss, former ambassador to Russia and a senior partner in Akin, Gump, Strauss, Hauer & Feld; and John Swearingen, retired chairman of Standard Oil Company of

Ted Forstmann, a founding partner of Forstmann Little & Company, is the master of the leveraged buyout. When he heard Gulfstream was for sale, he wasted no time in securing a meeting with Allen Paulson. *(Photo courtesy of Gulfstream Aerospace.)*

Indiana (now Amoco) and former chairman of Continental Bank.

Many of these directors were part of Forstmann Little's advisory group, which included the firm's investors. As the last decade of the 20th century began, the clouds quickly darkened over Gulfstream Aerospace, and many of these directors would strongly suggest — even demand — that Ted Forstmann cut his losses and get rid of Gulfstream; Forstmann had underestimated the amount of work Gulfstream needed, and now the company was heavily leveraged, facing rising competition and an economy spiraling downward.

"It was supposed to be just another LBO," wrote Kadlec. "Cut some costs. Sell a few more jets. But it wouldn't work out that way. The hard part was just beginning, and no one knew it."[34]

1990
Worldwide recession begins.

1991
William Lowe is appointed president and COO to reverse Gulfstream's declining sales.

1992
A $100 million IPO fails to generate investor interest. Gulfstream withdraws the IPO. The company is running out of cash.

1992
The GIV-SP replaces the GIV. Meanwhile, Gulfstream announces selection of the BMW/Rolls-Royce BR710 for the GV.

1992
Allen Paulson steps down as chairman and CEO. William Lowe succeeds him.

1993
Fred Breidenbach joins as president and COO. Chris Davis becomes Chief Financial Officer.

1993
Ted Forstmann replaces Lowe and becomes chairman and de facto CEO.

1993
Gulfstream announces that the GIV-SP and the GV will be built concurrently, the first time two models are produced together.

1994
W.W. "Bill" Boisture is hired as a senior vice president.

1994
Pres Henne is hired to continue the GV development effort. Charles Coppi steps aside. Joe Lombardo is hired to run the coproduction programs.

1995
Gulfstream Shares program is launched with Executive Jet International to sell fractional shares in GIVs. That year, Executive Jet orders seven aircraft.

1995
Gulfstream Aircraft Inc. and Gulfstream Financial Services are initiated by Chris Davis.

1995
Bombardier's Bryan Moss is hired to be vice chairman of Gulfstream Aerospace and CEO of Gulfstream Aircraft.

1995
The first flight of the GV takes place in November.

1996
Gulfstream sells 28 million shares in a successful IPO.

1997
Gulfstream Aerospace wins the Robert J. Collier Trophy for the GV.

1998
Gulfstream Aerospace buys K-C Aviation. The company also launches Gulfstream Charter Services, Gulfstream Lease and Gulfstream Management Services.

1998
Revenue and earnings continue to break records. By the end of the year, revenue tops $2.4 billion with $225 million in earnings.

1999
General Dynamics buys Gulfstream for $5.3 billion.

Gen. "Stormin'" Norman Schwarzkopf steps off a GIII (designated C-20 by the military) at a Saudi Arabian airport. GIIIs were used exten-
sively by military and political leaders throughout the Gulf War. *(Photo courtesy of Gulfstream Aerospace.)*

CHAPTER TEN

BATTLE FOR THE SKIES

1990–1995

*"The question we asked was, 'Can this be reversed?' My recommen-
dation ... was, yes, it could be, because the product was still great.
Management had done everything wrong, but Gulfstream still had a
great business and the product hadn't lost its edge."*

— Sandra Horbach, on her analysis
of Gulfstream's darkest hours[1]

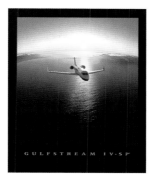

GULFSTREAM IV-SP

AFTER TED FORSTMANN CLOSED the deal on Gulfstream, he left the company in the hands of his partner, Brian Little, and Allen Paulson. From the outset, Forstmann intended to involve Paulson to a much greater degree than Chrysler had. It was one of the criteria the Forstmann Little firm sought in its acquisitions. They wanted a company with a dominant brand, growth potential and good management. In this case, the firm had the advantage of retaining the man who originally built up Gulfstream Aerospace. Paulson was charged with cutting costs and boosting sales.

The playing field, however, had changed. Dassault and Bombardier's Canadair were developing airplanes to match or exceed the performance of the GIV. Dassault had the Falcon 900 series, which, the company claimed, had better performance than the GIV. Its actual performance fell below expectations, but the triple-engine jet was nevertheless carving a niche in between the Canadair Challenger and the Gulfstream IV in terms of cabin size, comfort and price.

Bombardier was particularly aggressive. In 1986, the company had purchased Canadair from the Canadian government, which had already sunk $2 billion into the initial development of an ultra-long-range jet. Within four years, Bombardier snapped up struggling aviation manufacturers DeHavilland, Learjet and Short Brothers. These acquisitions catapulted Bombardier to eminence as one of the world's largest makers of aircraft for the commuter airline market and corporate air fleets.[2] By 1992, the company began the process of developing an aircraft destined to be called the Global Express, a clear challenge to Gulfstream's leadership position. Moreover, the company fielded an impressive executive team that played to win.

Then there was the economy, which, after eight years of growth, slid into a recession in 1990. Corporations began to restructure themselves to become more competitive globally, which led to massive layoffs of both blue- and white-collar workers.

This restructuring set the stage for an unprecedented economic boom. Like scattered seeds, displaced workers would soon sprout their own businesses, seizing on the opportunities afforded by burgeoning technologies such as the Internet. But in 1990, layoffs and the recession had led to widespread criticism of "corporate excess," and the corporate jet once again became a convenient tar-

The GIV-SP, an improved version of the GIV, kept Gulfstream ahead of the competition in performance, but the company was beginning to face a stiff fight for market share. *(Photo courtesy of Gulfstream Aerospace.)*

get of pundits who ignored its proven value as a tool of business. That year a so-called luxury tax was enacted, adding 10 percent to the purchase price of airplanes and boats.[3]

A 1990 *New York Times* analysis of the corporate aircraft market noted that there was a drop in fuel sales for corporate aviation, suggesting that companies were already using their jets less. Nevertheless, the piece asserted, sales of Gulfstream jets were surprisingly stable and the company was continuing to perform well.

The reality was different. Firm orders were evaporating, and new orders were increasingly hard to come by. By the end of 1990, orders had fallen from 29 to 21, and the company still had to meet interest payments on the $700 million debt — about $70 million a year.[4]

At Gulfstream, Paulson started to tighten the belt to deal with the decreasing number of orders. In April, approximately 200 contract employees, or "jobshoppers," were eliminated.[5] In a letter to employees, Paulson wrote:

> "After delivering a record 49 Gulfstream IV aircraft in 1988 and 32 aircraft in 1989, Gulfstream projects 32 deliveries in 1990. This fact alone necessitates our taking a very hard look at our company and how it now runs."[6]

In addition to the layoffs, employees' cost-of-living raises were stopped. In another letter sent to employees, Paulson explained that "we have taken on heavy debt which necessitates our delaying development of any new products in the next couple of years."[7]

These actions were not enough, and this was just the beginning of what would become some very dark days for Gulfstream Aerospace. These ever-gloomier economic reports, however, were soon to be overshadowed by Gulfstream's important contributions to another cause in the late summer of 1990.

On Duty in the Gulf War

On August 2, Saddam Hussein, President of Iraq sent more than 100,000 troops into neighboring Kuwait, the beginning of a nearly year-long deadly drama. As history has recorded, an international coalition of forces led by the United States responded quickly to meet this threat to world security. In a very short time, the United States alone deployed more than half a million troops and their weapons, support equipment and other supplies to Saudi Arabia.

When it became clear that a diplomatic solution could not be found, the coalition forces

The GIII's short-field capability was crucial because Iraqi forces littered the runway of Kuwait International Airport with debris, shortening the field by 3,000 feet. The GIII pictured here landed following the expulsion of Iraqi forces from Kuwait. Smoke from burning oil wells is visible in the background. *(Photo courtesy of Gulfstream Aerospace.)*

The USAF C-20B, a Gulfstream GIII equipped with a high-frequency tail antenna. The C-20s were used during Operation Desert Storm and Operation Desert Sabre to fly high-ranking military officials all over the Middle East.

turned "Operation Desert Shield" to the now historic "Operation Desert Storm" on January 18, 1991. Night after night, the world witnessed an air offensive never seen before, which combined technology, skill and sheer heroism into a devastating assault on Iraqi command and control centers, armored units and air defense sites.

On February 23, the long-awaited ground assault — called Operation Desert Sabre — began with the famous "Hail Mary" maneuver, in which tanks and troops secretly moved 120 miles to the west to flank Hussein's formidable defense line and attack Iraqi armored divisions from the rear. Within 100 hours, the ground war was over. The Iraqi army, stunned by weeks of continuous bombing, surrendered by the thousands, some even giving themselves up to journalists, who were unsure what to do with their insistent captives.

For well-deserved and obvious reasons, media coverage of the war focused heavily on tactical aircraft and their air crews. But as noted after the war in the company magazine, the *Gulfstreamer*, "virtually every type of military transport aircraft participated to some extent throughout the crisis, and with equally exemplary records of accomplishments."[8]

In fact, some of the first U.S. military aircraft to fly into the region were GIIIs (designated C-20s by the military) that comprised part of the 58th Military Airlift Squadron. On August 6, 1990, four days after Iraq's invasion, GIIIs carried high level U.S. government officials all over the Middle East. It was they who coordinated support among the various Arab nations and forged an unlikely alliance against Iraq's aggression.

On August 21, a GIII was assigned to General Norman Schwarzkopf. From that day until April 1991, a GIII stood ready to transport the commander and his staff 24 hours a day, seven days a week. The GIIIs served as a flying office for the general and his staff. Air crews worked under difficult conditions. Under the occasional Scud missile attack, they kept the aircraft operating continuously in 100-degree-plus temperatures. No airplane was damaged from missiles or falling debris.[9]

On the political front, Gulfstream aircraft permitted government and military chiefs to meet face-to-face with members of the coalition, which kept the alliance together. They also made frequent trips to Israel because, early in the war, Hussein began lobbing Scud missiles at the Jewish nation to provoke retaliation in the hope of splintering the alliance.

After the cease-fire was declared, Gulfstream aircraft — mostly GIIIs — were used to survey the ecological and structural damage caused by the Iraqis during their occupation of Kuwait. Here, the airplane's short-field performance was crucial. A pilot landing at the remains of Kuwait

International Airport described the conditions in a letter to Gulfstream Aerospace:

"We landed on that runway which had only about 5,000 feet open. The last 3,000 feet still had junk cars, concrete construction barriers and other debris that the Iraqis had dragged out on the runways and taxiways to keep us off."[10]

In the almost eight months of Operation Desert Shield and Desert Storm, Gulfstreams from the Army, Air Force, Marines and Coast Guard flew a combined 250,000 nautical miles on various military and political missions. Not a single departure was missed because of an airplane-related problem.

Gulfstream aircraft, noted the *Gulfstreamer* magazine, "took America's military and government leaders where they needed to be in order to be most effective — first, in managing the crisis, then in managing the war."

"Those challenges may be history, but the Gulfstream aircraft at work for our nation have had little time to reflect on all that they helped accomplish. Now they are involved in helping America shape and manage the peace."[11]

A Struggle Closer to Home

Gulfstream employees were proud of their contributions to the war effort, but they were still facing an uncertain future. Prodded by world events and the rising price of fuel, the economy in the United States finally toppled into a brief yet intense recession. This time Gulfstream was not spared. Paulson's cost cutting was not effective because the real issue — efficiency — was something that had not been addressed. "Gulfstream had always been an engineering-driven company in which product quality was valued for more than efficiency," noted a *Business Week* article.

"And why not? For decades, the company had had no real competition."[12]

As revenues dropped, Ted Forstmann persuaded Allen Paulson that it was time to bring in some new blood at the top. A lengthy and frustrating executive search ensued. After eight months Forstmann Little chose William Lowe, a marketing executive who had worked at IBM and Xerox. Lowe, who became president and COO of Gulfstream in 1991, had no experience in the aviation industry. According to *Georgia Trend* magazine, Lowe "sheepishly admits the sum total of his piloting experience consists of crashing the company's test simulator at Savannah International Airport."[13] He was chosen to reenergize sales, bring costs into line and basically reclaim the title as the undisputed leader of the business jet market.

The year Lowe joined Gulfstream as president, the company recorded a stunning loss of almost $50 million (and still less than half the loss recorded in 1990). Paulson was gradually receding into the background, but he nevertheless clashed with Lowe immediately.

One of their disagreements concerned the fate of Paulson's pet project, the supersonic business jet, that was being developed jointly with Sukhoi, the Russian aircraft manufacturer. Lowe, who was appointed CEO in early 1992, won. He shelved the program later that year, and the money saved from the program was to go into development of a new ultra-long-range aircraft, the GV. But Lowe spent much of the savings on adding sales personnel and an improved version called the GIV-SP. The SP stood for "Special Performance." Industry commentators immediately dubbed it "Same Plane." In fact, the GIV-SP breathed new life in the GIV program.

A marketing pro, Lowe believed the way to sell airplanes was to spend more money on advertising. That approach may work well for a division

Left and above: The GIV-SP had a maximum customer useful load (payload and interior allowance) some 53 percent higher than the GIV. Cabin width was also increased. Traditionally, one product line ended when another began, but the decision was made in 1993 to continue producing the GIV-SP line along with the new GV that was in development. *(Photo courtesy of Gulfstream Aerospace.)*

In early 1993, after Fred Breidenbach was named president of Gulfstream, he recruited Chris Davis, below, a 17-year veteran of General Electric, as the company's CFO. A year later, Bill Boisture, right, joined the company. A decorated Vietnam War veteran, Boisture brought solid business aviation experience to Gulfstream.

of a large company with other sources of cash flow, but Gulfstream didn't have that kind of money.

Paulson was also incensed by Lowe's decision to discount sale prices of GIVs. "When he started doing that, I just about died," Paulson said. "It opened the way to haggling."[14] Worse still, the costs of research and development, administration and marketing soared.

Fewer new airplanes were being ordered. Those that had been sold were discounted even though costs were rising and sales contracts had easy exit provisions. Moreover, there was no focus on selling aircraft traded in for new GIVs. These used aircraft amounted to $180 million in potential revenue that was simply eating up hangar space.

To raise money for the new GV program, Gulfstream launched a $100 million IPO in early 1992. It was, as Forstmann and others candidly acknowledged, an utter failure. In the opinion of Sandra Horbach, a Forstmann Little partner, it was a blessing that the IPO failed. "Thank God the IPO failed because the follow-on would have been a disaster," she said. The company had few orders backlogged and an ill-defined plan for going forward.[15]

The financial numbers, as writer Daniel Kadlec noted in his book, *Masters of the Universe*, were "far too rosy and could have been deemed grossly misleading."[16] Furthermore, the cost projections for the GV weren't realistic. In short, as Horbach explained in a 1999 interview, "the board was not getting an accurate picture. The numbers were getting worse, but the presentation given to the board kept getting better."[17]

Allen Paulson, meanwhile, had withdrawn completely from management of the company. In the summer of 1992, after the supersonic jet project was canceled, Paulson cleaned out his office and put his 10,000-square-foot Greek Revival mansion up for sale. That fall Forstmann bought out Paulson's stake for $50 million and invested another much needed $200 million in the company.

Paulson had left Gulfstream without fanfare. In an interview with a local magazine he said: "Either you run something or you're not running it. Being how I'm not running it, that's why I sold my interest. I'm the sort of guy that has to own and control it. If I can't, I want out."[18] He stepped down as chairman and remained on the board as a director and chairman emeritus. He was soon followed by Albert "Goldie" Glenn, who retired from active participation as well. Glenn remained a consultant with Gulfstream.

At Gulfstream, the turmoil continued. In December 1992, Lowe told the board that the company was on track to sell 28 to 30 GIVs by the end of 1992. The actual number was 25, which meant revenue projections were off by $60 million to $100 million, and costs still hadn't been reined in. Gulfstream lost another $50 million by year's end.[19]

Up until this point, Forstmann had been distracted. After he engineered Gulfstream's LBO, he had gone on to buy cable equipment maker General Instrument, a $1.7 billion LBO that was twice the size of Gulfstream. General Instrument had problems of its own, and Forstmann concentrated on resolving those, which he did with great success. His time was further pressed by serving as cochairman of President George Bush's reelection campaign.

Forstmann knew there were problems with Gulfstream, but he stuck to his proven practice of trusting his executives to turn things around. In

President George Bush boards a GIII — Air Force One. The designation Air Force One is given to any aircraft from the Air Force that the president is aboard. A Marine aircraft is known as Marine One, and so on. A near collision involving President Eisenhower's airplane led to this designation system. *(Photo courtesy of Gulfstream Aerospace.)*

A.H. "GOLDIE" GLENN

WHEN ALBERT "GOLDIE" GLENN WAS sent from Grumman's headquarters in Bethpage, New York, to Savannah in 1969, he figured he would spend a few years at this unwanted post and then head back to Long Island.

More than 20 years later, when he officially retired from the company, Glenn was still in Savannah and today lives in South Carolina.

Glenn, who joined Grumman in 1940 and steadily rose through the ranks of the company, grew up hanging out at Roosevelt Field, often called America's "cradle of aviation." From there, he watched Charles Lindbergh take off on his solo flight across the Atlantic Ocean in 1927. "I was a kid who hung around and emptied oil cans and wiped planes," Glenn told the *Savannah News-Press* in 1983. "I did anything just to be around them. It seems there was always something going on."[1]

Glenn attended the New York State Aircraft and Engineering School and went to work for Grumman as a riveter-assembler.

But that wasn't enough to satisfy his lust for aviation. He used his airframe license to get into the hangar and flight operations.[2] He worked on the F4F Wildcat and F6F Hellcat fighters during World War II, and after the war he performed modifications to Grumman's amphibious aircraft.[3] In 1946, he was assigned to the Blue Angels, the Navy's flight exhibition team, as a technical representative, and traveled the world with the elite flyers.

When he moved to Savannah, he was ready to settle down. "I think after having traveled for so long and having been involved in so many things, it was the right move," he said years later.[4]

In Savannah, he was put in charge of service and support for the Gulfstream aircraft. Throughout his career, he was promoted many times, serving as vice president and general manager of the Savannah facility, and eventually was named president of Gulfstream Aerospace. In 1993, when he retired, he was vice chairman of Gulfstream Aerospace, after already having served twice as president. On the occasion of his retirement, after 53 years of service, the company established the Goldie Glenn Scholarship Program in his honor. The award notes: "Goldie has always been proud of the fact that through self-education, hard work and help from many others he was able to progress from an airplane mechanic to the president of Gulfstream Aerospace Corporation.... This scholarship program is a tribute to Goldie and the outstanding leadership, service and respect that he brought to Gulfstream Aerospace Corporation."[5]

Fred Breidenbach was hired as president and COO of Gulfstream on April 1, 1993. A few days later, Breidenbach discovered that Gulfstream was within three months of running out of cash. *(Photo courtesy of Gulfstream Aerospace.)*

1993, he realized that the termites in the house of Gulfstream were ready to bring it crashing down.

The Pros

Forstmann turned to Gerard Roche, a member of the board who was also chairman of the well-known executive search firm Heidrick & Struggles, to find someone who could bring order from chaos. Roche responded with Fred Breidenbach, who was hired as president and chief operating officer. Until his decision to join Gulfstream, Breidenbach had spent his entire career at General Electric, joining the company after graduating from Penn State University in 1968. He rose through the ranks to become vice president and general manager of GE's 3,200-employee government Electronic Systems Division.

Forstmann told Breidenbach during their interview that Gulfstream needed someone to get the plant running more efficiently. Forstmann characterized the job as a turnaround from a fiscal standpoint, but neither Breidenbach nor Forstmann knew how bad the situation actually was. Breidenbach became president and chief operating officer on April 1, 1993, a date that sticks in his mind. Just a few days after he looked over the situation, Breidenbach discovered that Gulfstream was within 90 days of running out of cash.

Ted Forstmann and Sandra Horbach then hired Chris Davis, a 17-year veteran of GE, as the company's new executive vice president and chief financial officer. (Gulfstream's previous CFO was asked to resign in 1992. The position was left vacant until Davis stepped in.) Two weeks after her arrival, Davis had her first taste of what was in store for her that summer. After producing a detailed analysis, she prepared a board presentation that included an accurate but "ugly" financial forecast for 1993. She reviewed it with Lowe, who then told her to present 1993 with a forecast for 1994 that showed the situation was going to dramatically improve.

Davis responded: "I cannot present 1994 because we have no idea what 1994 is going to look like." Lowe insisted that they were going to present 1994, but Davis resisted.[20]

After further discussion, Lowe decided not to present a 1994 forecast to the board. After the board meeting, Davis met with Forstmann and Horbach and discussed outside support to analyze the business. Forstmann sent Horbach and several external consultants to Savannah to look over Gulfstream as if it were a new investment. "Tell me whether or not you would buy this company today," he told Horbach. All summer long, Horbach, Davis, four accountants and two lawyers poured over every invoice and contract. What they discovered, they said, violated every sound principle of business. They discovered that there was no budget. Money was spent without regard to the actual financial condition of the company. If sales forecasts didn't justify an expenditure, the forecasts were simply revised upward.[21]

"There was a thing called a "request for budget adjustment," recalled Davis, "which was, if you didn't have enough money or you didn't like

The Gulfstream C-20G was built for the U.S. Navy and delivered
on February 4, 1994. More orders soon followed. Interestingly,
this aircraft has a cargo door that enables the plane to carry
three pallets or 26 passengers or a combination of pallets and
passengers. *(Photo courtesy of Gulfstream Aerospace.)*

the budget you had, you'd come in and request 'an adjustment to your budget.' There was a form somebody filled out and signed, and then your budget changed."[22]

Horbach said there was one saving grace: Gulfstream's product. "The product ultimately allowed the company to be saved because it was such a fabulous product," she said.

"The question we asked was, 'Can this be reversed?' My recommendation to Ted was, yes, it could be, because the product was still great. Management had done everything wrong, but Gulfstream still had a great business and the product hadn't lost its edge."[23]

However, in the early part of 1993, seven of these airplanes had stacked up on the tarmac as customers canceled their orders, Gulfstream ran out of cash and was on the brink of violating its loan covenants. Horbach, using Forstmann Little's reputation, met with the banks, persuaded them to grant waivers and introduced them to Davis. Davis then kept the banks well informed, something that had not been done in the past. She wrote letters providing the banks with a monthly update of the business, Gulfstream's strategy and financial information. With a plan in hand, the company began to rebuild its credibility.

Meanwhile, Breidenbach cut back the production schedule, and Gulfstream offered voluntary separation packages. Through early retirements and resignations, about 750 people left the company. Many of the resignations occurred in the management ranks because Breidenbach discovered that Gulfstream had too many managerial layers. The company also cut back on discretionary spending. Training programs, building projects and advertising were either reduced or put on hold.

Breidenbach and Davis' cost-cutting sent a signal that Gulfstream was serious in trying to right the financial ship. They overrode concerns that by cutting back, Gulfstream was admitting weakness, which could hurt sales. Possibly the most realistic perspective was found on the shop floor among the hourly workers. Every time a Gulfstream was ordered, a flag was raised. When they toured the factory to explain the reasons for the cutbacks, they received this response from the workers: "Well, I'm not surprised. We haven't seen many flags."

"It was a very mature reaction," Breidenbach noted. "We had much less resistance in the hourly people than we did with the management crew in understanding what we were doing."[24] Breidenbach and Davis were able to cut $50 million in expenses in 1993, but that was not enough to forestall a loss of $275 million that year. Forstmann had had enough and fired Bill Lowe that November.

On the Line

Ted Forstmann's next step was perhaps the most controversial in a career filled with remarkably successful risks. He rejected the advice of his friends and investors who told him to dump Gulfstream, take the hit — a $600 million hit by most accounts — and move on with his life. Instead, he assumed the role of chairman and de facto chief executive. Forstmann did not assume the actual title because he believed a CEO should live near the corporate headquarters. Forstmann remained in New York, conferring with Breidenbach, Davis and others via telephone and weekly visits. His reasons for refusing to admit defeat were myriad. Forstmann's reputation, he said, was on the line, and he did not believe the firm could have survived if he sold out. But more than that, he recognized that there was a tremendous esprit de corps in the Gulfstream organization. Forstmann refused to give up on that fighting spirit.

Close friends continued to try to talk him out of it. Robert Strauss, the former ambassador to Russia and an integral part of the Forstmann Little advisory group, told him point blank that "We've made a bum deal, and you ought to get out of it, the quicker the better." Strauss tried to enlist the help of George Shultz, the former secretary of state, and Nick Forstmann, Ted Forstmann's brother and partner in the firm, to persuade him to dump Gulfstream. But as Strauss recalled, Forstmann was "hellbent" on turning the company around.

By now, Forstmann Little had invested a total of $450 million in Gulfstream from the subordinated debt fund. Forstmann moved quickly to convert the entire debt to preferred stock. That immediately eliminated $38 million a year in interest payments to the firm's investors, a move that further frustrated the backers of Forstmann Little. The investors had granted Forstmann sole discretion to manage their money, so they had no choice in the matter. Nevertheless, he visited them to win their moral support and endured their criticisms. "I did not think we were wrong to buy the company," Forstmann said.

"So I just said, 'I can do it.' We are going to turn this around. It became a huge bet because if it hadn't worked, we would have been finished."[25]

The criticisms only stiffened Forstmann's resolve. "As soon as someone tells Ted something can't be done, you've challenged him to the task," Chris Davis explained.[26]

Meanwhile, Breidenbach and Davis were tapping the gray matter to come up with new cost-cutting ideas. "We talked to everyone, including the employees who were closest to it," said Breidenbach.

"They have wonderfully good ideas if anyone would listen to them. We forced that process into

brainstorming groups captained by ... an engineer or an hourly worker — whoever had those leadership skills."[27]

Since Forstmann, Horbach and the new leadership team decided to keep the GIV-SP in production (the first time Gulfstream would produce two products in its history), the company also launched what Breidenbach called the "Tin Cup Campaign." Breidenbach visited with Gulfstream's major suppliers to renegotiate long-term agreements on the GIV to bring the costs down. Many of the suppliers — like Rolls-Royce for instance — had enjoyed a long

Friends and investors told Ted Forstmann that he had to get rid of Gulfstream and just swallow the loss. Forstmann refused and instead took the reins, installed a new management team and turned Gulfstream around. Below are the members of the team. From left to right: William Boisture, Sandra Horbach, Ted Forstmann and Chris Davis. *(Photo courtesy of Gulfstream Aerospace.)*

and prosperous relationship with Gulfstream since the airplane's inception in the 1950s. Likewise, a deep reservoir of trust existed between Gulfstream and its suppliers. When it came time to tap the reservoir, Breidenbach had to convince them the GIV-SP would stay in production, and eventually succeeded far beyond his imagination. "We called it the Tin Cup Campaign because we had no intention to try to threaten them," Breidenbach explained. Gulfstream needed their help in the long term.

"We weren't going to say, 'If you don't reduce your price on this subassembly we're going to give this to someone else.' That was a very hollow threat, as it would have been with all the other major components. Instead, we told them what has been happening with the price of the GIV, a picture of a line going up each year. 'Here's what our costs have been doing and it parallels the price line, and by the way, Mr. Supplier, here is what your prices have been doing.' All the lines were amazingly parallel, each one going up from left to right. And we showed the corresponding market share, and that was going down."[28]

Breidenbach successfully reduced the price, in some cases by double digits, on multi-year contracts, a move that was key in turning Gulfstream around. As a sign of appreciation, Gulfstream gave the chairmen and senior executives of these companies plaques embedded with tin cups.

Costs were coming under control, but there was still the matter of selling off the trade-ins. In December 1993, Chris Davis personally inspected these idle aircraft. When the sales manager for pre-owned inventory opened the door to the first airplane, Davis was greeted with the stale odor of abandonment. "It was like going into an old house that has flocked wallpaper in it," she recalled.[29] Davis decided to take some risk and put money into the used aircraft to refurbish the interiors. The program was called "New Again": Trade-ins were refurbished and sold again under a limited warranty.

When W.W. "Bill" Boisture, today president and COO of Gulfstream, was hired in February 1994, he established an incentive program to encourage the entire sales force to sell off these airplanes. A revised commission plan encouraged the sales force to sell a trade-in before it even arrived at Gulfstream.

Boisture's path to Gulfstream is unique because he sought out Forstmann rather than the other way around. A former Air Force pilot who had won the Distinguished Flying Cross during Vietnam, Boisture had had a career that spanned the military and the civilian side of aviation. Like many former military pilots, he developed a passion for the business aviation industry and had been involved with Canadair's Challenger business jet program. "I wanted to be in a business where there was a direct correlation between products and services and the impact they had on the customer," he said. "Business aviation is a very exciting place because of that."[30]

In the fall of 1993, Boisture had finished consolidating British Aerospace's Hawker aircraft business to sell it to Raytheon. Mission accomplished, Boisture looked for the next opportunity and heard that Forstmann was searching for key executives. Anxious to meet someone of Forstmann's reputation, Boisture called the executive search firm to meet with the headhunter. The headhunter was preparing to leave for an overseas trip, but Boisture wrangled a 30-minute interview in the firm's office. Two and a half hours later, the headhunter called Forstmann and said he ought to talk with Boisture. Later that afternoon the two men sat down for an interview. Boisture recalled that at one point during the interview Forstmann sat upright in his chair and asked, "How did you get here again?"[31] From that day on, Forstmann often referred to Boisture as the "walk on" player on his turnaround team.

Besides securing new orders and selling the used inventory, Boisture embarked on improving a third area: "We needed to start building, for the long term, a market-leading, winning attitude in the company," he said.

"It was important to convince this group of people that they were not going to get beat by Bombardier and that we were going to win. It was a market this company had created, and we were gong to sustain the leadership position regardless of what was coming out of our competitors in Canada."[32]

Boisture was alluding to Bombardier's Global Express, which was introduced shortly after Gulfstream announced the new GV. The Global Express was an obvious shot across Gulfstream's

WHERE EXPERIENCE COUNTS

BESIDES HIS EXECUTIVE TEAM, Forstmann gathered a board of directors unique in the history of business. Pictured in 1996, the board possessed expertise that cut across industry, business, politics, management and technology. It set a high standard for Gulfstream to meet. *(Photos courtesy of Gulfstream Aerospace.)*

William R. Acquavella
President,
Acquavella Galleries, Inc.

Robert Anderson
Chairman Emeritus,
Rockwell International
Corporation

Charlotte L. Beers
Chairman,
J. Walter Thompson
Chairman Emeritus,
Ogilvy & Mather Worldwide

Thomas D. Bell, Jr.
Chairman & CEO,
Burson-Marsteller

W.W. Boisture, Jr.
President & COO,
Gulfstream Aerospace
Corporation

Fred A. Breidenbach
Former President & COO,
Gulfstream Aerospace
Corporation

Chris A. Davis
Executive Vice President & Chief
Financial & Administrative Officer,
Gulfstream Aerospace Corporation

Lynn Forester
Co-Chief Executive Officer,
FirstMark Holdings, Inc.

Nicholas C. Forstmann
Founding General Partner,
Forstmann Little & Co.

Theodore J. Forstmann
Chairman & CEO,
Gulfstream Aerospace Corporation
Founding General Partner,
Forstmann Little & Co.

Sandra J. Horbach
General Partner,
Forstmann Little & Co.

James T. Johnson
Former President & COO,
Gulfstream Aerospace
Corporation

Henry A. Kissinger
Chairman,
Kissinger Associates, Inc.
Former U.S. Secretary
of State

Drew Lewis
Former Chairman & CEO,
Union Pacific Corporation

Mark H. McCormack
Chairman, President & CEO,
International Management
Group

Bryan T. Moss
Vice Chairman,
Gulfstream Aerospace
Corporation

Michael S. Ovitz
CKE Investments
Artists Management Group
Former Chairman,
Creative Artists Agency

Allen E. Paulson
Chairman Emeritus,
Gulfstream Aerospace
Corporation

Roger S. Penske
Chairman,
Penske Corporation

Colin L. Powell
Chairman, America's Promise—
The Alliance for Youth
Former Chairman,
U.S. Joint Chiefs of Staff

Gerard R. Roche
Chairman,
Heidrick & Struggles, Inc.

Donald H. Rumsfeld
Chairman,
Gilead Sciences, Inc.
Former U.S. Secretary of Defense

George P. Shultz
Former U.S. Secretary
of State

Robert S. Strauss
Founder & Partner,
Akin, Gump, Strauss, Hauer & Feld
Former U.S. Ambassador to Russia

bow because on paper it matched the specs of the GV. Both were billed as ultra-long-distance jets capable of nonstop flight from New York to Tokyo. On paper, the specs appeared at first glance to be similar, even to the point that Bombardier followed Gulfstream's lead and selected the same BMW/Rolls-Royce engines.

This was the beginning of what *Business Week* called "trench warfare" between the two sales organizations. "Gulfstream and Canadair [owned by Bombardier] sales forces fanned out around the world seeking advance orders from every corporation, government agency and high-rolling entrepreneur with $35 million to spend."[33]

Bombardier, which had revenues of almost $5 billion in 1993, was putting a lot on the line with the Global Express. Besides the research and development costs, Bombardier planned to put its name to the aircraft, a first for a company heretofore known mainly for its lines of recreational craft such as the Sea Doo and snowmobiles. A Canadian magazine called *Canadian Business* depicted the struggle as a classic "David and Goliath struggle.... But here's the kicker: Goliath hails from Canada."[34]

Where Experience Counts

Forstmann was determined to win. Like a corporate version of King Arthur, he unsheathed his broadsword and entered the sales fray, battling for every order as if the company depended upon it — which it did. Gulfstream reengineered its advertising campaign, adopting a more aggressive tone. He challenged competitors' assertions that for the price, customers did not need a Gulfstream. One ad played on that theme. With a picture of the Aspen runway and the mountains as the background, a tag line read: "If you don't need a Gulfstream, you shouldn't buy one."

Another ad showed the crumpled nose of a Global Express, depicted as a paper airplane, with the tag line, "Canadair will still be making promises when we're making airplanes." Forstmann also adopted the theme that Gulfstream was in effect a private company competing against foreign government-subsidized airplane manufacturers — Bombardier and Dassault.

Forstmann did not fight this war alone. Since he took the reins of Gulfstream, he had been

putting together a board of directors unique in the history of business. In addition to his senior executives, the men and women who became part of this executive round table included Roger Penske, longtime friend of Forstmann and chairman and CEO of Penske Corporation; George Shultz, former secretary of state; Bob Anderson, chairman emeritus of Rockwell Corporation; William Acquavella, president of Acquavella Galleries; Drew Lewis, former chairman and CEO of Union Pacific Corporation; Michael Ovitz, former chairman and co-owner of Creative Artists Agency and onetime Disney executive; Charlotte Beers, chairman emeritus of Ogilvy & Mather Worldwide; Mark McCormack, chairman, president and CEO of International Management Group; Sandra Horbach, partner with Forstmann Little; Nicholas Forstmann, founding partner in the Forstmann Little firm; Robert Strauss, former U.S. ambassador to Russia and founder and partner of Akin, Gump, Strauss, Hauer & Feld; Lynn Forester, president and CEO of FirstMark Holdings; Gerard Roche, chairman of Heidrick & Struggles; and Tom Bell, president and CEO of Burson-Marsteller. By 1996, the roundtable would include former Secretary of State Henry Kissinger; Colin Powell, former chairman of the Joints Chiefs of Staff; Donald Rumsfeld, former secretary of defense; and James Johnson, who would briefly become Gulfstream president and COO.

Boisture noted that the presence of so many incredibly accomplished individuals did more for Gulfstream than provide access to business and national leaders around the world. "The members of our board are people who have very high standards for everything they get involved in," he said.

"They set the bar for effort and set it pretty high because these people were willing to put their reputations with ours. They demanded excellent business performance, which was great because that's the way to do things."[35]

A telling example of this occurred in 1996, after Marsha Grovenstein became vice president of customer service. She went to dinner one night with a number of executives and directors and found herself sitting next to Roger Penske. "He had a lot of support-related questions," she recalled. "He looked me squarely in the face and

Employees knew how dire Gulfstream's situation was in the early 1990s. They pitched in to find ways to improve efficiency and cut costs. *(Photo courtesy of Gulfstream Aerospace.)*

said, 'OK, I buy one of these things. I take it home with me. Now what happens to me?' We talked for three hours on the service structure."

Tom Bell, vice chairman of Gulfstream from 1993 to 1995, said each board member was there because of Forstmann. "He recruited every one of them himself, and he recruited each individual for a reason," Bell explained. "I always tell people that going to a Gulfstream board meeting is like going to a cabinet meeting."[36] Michael Ovitz agreed. "One of the fun things about going to a Gulfstream meeting was being around this brain power," he said. "The room was a little frightening."[37]

Each board member contributed more than his or her name. They became involved with the discussions of the GV program, its mission require-

ments, funding issues and service. They also comprised a sales force second to none. "Ultimately, Gulfstream is about selling quality airplanes to quality buyers," explained Ovitz. "The people in that board room had relationships across almost every industry, from banking to entertainment, to oil transportation, to the military, etc. The board's composition was incredibly well thought through."[38]

The board provided access to the decision maker — the first tier. Previously, the sales organization had tried to sell the corporate pilot or aviation director on the Gulfstream aircraft. But, as Forstmann pointed out, "no flight department has ever bought a plane in the history of the world. They don't have the capital."

The flight department's personnel could block a sale, however, because they are the ones who ultimately fly and maintain the aircraft. The second-tier approach involved winning over the department, which wasn't hard to do once you put a qualified pilot behind the yoke of a Gulfstream. Chris Davis said Forstmann "understood how CEOs felt about airplanes, and he understood how to strategically leverage the board to help our sales teams to get doors open for them."[39]

Sharing Growth

The strategy was clearly working. By the end of 1994, less than a year after Forstmann assumed control of Gulfstream, the aviation company posted a record $46 million in profit on revenues of more than $900 million, as compared to three consecutive years of losses.

Ken Burckhardt, senior vice president of finance who joined Gulfstream in December 1994, recalled asking Boisture how the year was going to wind up. "We had something like 20 orders, but we were expecting 40," said Burckhardt. "I asked him, 'Are we going to make our numbers?' He said we would. Damn if we didn't do it."[40]

Gulfstream had landed its largest order in its history — a half-billion-dollar order from Executive Jet Aviation (EJA). The order not only broke Gulfstream records, it was the largest order in the history of the business jet industry, according to the General Aviation Manufacturers Association.[41]

The unprecedented order for 20 GIVs and two GVs was the result of a strategic partnership

formed with EJA's chairman, Richard Santulli. Santulli was a pioneer of the NetJet concept, in which customers could buy fractional shares in an aircraft in return for a certain number of hours of flight time. This gave customers access to a modern corporate jet without paying the whole acquisition price or maintenance fees.

Santulli and Boisture had done business together before. When Boisture was responsible for Butler Aviation in the late '80s, EJA had been his largest customer. And at British Aerospace the two had struck a deal that introduced mid-size jets to Santulli's growing business. The deal they struck at Gulfstream would later result in significant growth for both companies.

Launched in 1987, the fractional ownership concept was at first resisted by the sales organizations of aircraft manufacturers. They felt it would draw off those willing to buy and operate airplanes. Far from it, NetJet gave companies access to corporate jet travel that they otherwise would not have been able to afford. It also introduced these growing companies to the experience of business aviation without forcing them to first pay the steep entry fee. As the company prospered, it gained experience in corporate aviation to perhaps form its own flight department, if needed.

The partnership struck by Boisture and Santulli resulted in a fractional shares program, called "Gulfstream Shares," which worked with

Left: Four generations of Gulfstreams welcome the GV during rollout ceremonies. *(Photo courtesy of Charles Coppi.)*

Below: Affectionately known as "Mr. Gulfstream," Charles Coppi played a vital part in the development of every Gulfstream. He has been honored with the FAA's Distinguished Service Medal, AIAA's Aircraft Design Award and NBAA's Meritorious Service to Aviation Award. *(Photo courtesy of Gulfstream Aerospace.)*

an extension of EJA called Executive Jet International (EJI). The program included Gulfstream's commitment to provide a core fleet of used GIVs that, in the beginning, assisted in providing enough aircraft so a customer could request an airplane within hours before boarding the plane.

Becoming involved with the NetJet program was risky, recalled Boisture. "We had to come up with a business transaction and structure that would allow capital formation to make this sort of program work in its early stages," he said. "We also developed a unique maintenance program in which Gulfstream was responsible to EJI for the upkeep of the fleet."[42]

Meanwhile, Chris Davis had initiated another new program for the company: Gulfstream Financial Services. "One of the things I kept hearing from the sales managers is, 'I could sell more airplanes if we had financing options,'" said Davis. Gulfstream was not in a position to finance the airplanes itself, but Davis embarked upon negotiating private-label relationships with different financing institutions. In one year, Gulfstream went from having no financing options in its history to financing close to $300 million.

The coproduction of the GIV and GV presented some welcome challenges, namely, how to build and service both the GIV and the GV, which was approaching the rollout and first flight that would lead to certification. "We met that challenge by bringing in some good talent," Boisture said. Joe Lombardo arrived later in 1995 from McDonnell Douglas to lead the coproduction effort. He began to rearrange the way the factory was set up to speed up the process without sacrificing quality. Funds were also approved for a $16 million service center, giving Gulfstream the capacity to service a dozen more GVs at a time.

The stream of Gulfstream's new products and services owed itself, to a large degree, to how the company worked internally. In the past, Gulfstream was very rigid in its structure, explained Marsha Grovenstein. Vice presidents and directors of various departments rarely sat down with each other to attack a problem or crisis as a company. "If I had a budget problem or a technical problem in my organization, it was mine to figure out," she said. "There wasn't a holistic view. When Ted and his management team came in, integration among the departments became the rule rather than the exception."[43]

Gulfstream was still on the upswing, but Forstmann was not satisfied. "Ted isn't into ties or losing," Boisture recalled. "He asked 'What else can we do to beat these guys.' I said something along the lines of 'Short of hiring their leader, I'm not sure what else we can do right now.'"

The two men decided that was the next step and targeted Bryan Moss, the president of Bombardier's business jet division. Boisture had worked with Moss in the late seventies at Canadair. He gave him a call to broach the question. Moss was taken aback; the last thing he expected was a phone call from his competitor offering him a job. But the fact that it was

On September 22, 1995, the GV emerged amid a cloud of fog.
Despite the obstacles, the aircraft was completed on time.
Georgia Governor Zell Miller and FAA Administrator David
Hinson were among those on hand for the ceremony. *(Photo
courtesy of Gulfstream Aerospace.)*

Boisture making the call meant a lot to Moss. "Of all the people I've ever worked with, I have as much respect for Bill as an individual as anybody," Moss said. "So when I got the call from him, that was the first thing to set the hook."

Moss was the president of Bombardier's business aircraft division, a fierce competitor who was highly respected throughout the industry. Moss spearheaded Bombardier's challenge to Gulfstream's leadership position, embodied in the Global Express. "Those were heady times," recalled Moss.

"To put the Global Express into perspective, I'd been preaching for as long as I can remember the family-of-product strategy. The Global Express basically rounded out the line. We had Lear in the small segment and Challengers in the medium but nothing in the Gulfstream area. The Global Express completed the strategy by putting us in, up until then, what had been only Gulfstream territory." [44]

Moss thought that working for Gulfstream was an exciting way for him to cap his career. "What sold me was the combination of the financial aspects, the position and the opportunity to spend some time with the company that — I had to admit — had the best brand recognition and the best customer loyalty," Moss said. [45] He became vice chairman of Gulfstream, assuming that role from Tom Bell, who had been temporarily filling in and who remained on the board of directors.

Moss was also named chief executive of a new subsidiary that had been established in March. Called Gulfstream Aircraft, the new subsidiary was focused on the customer and charged with all marketing, sales, completions, product support and service functions worldwide.

In conjunction with the new subsidiary, a parts distribution operation was set up in Bahrain to support Gulfstream operations in the Middle East, Africa and surrounding regions. The center joined a growing number of overseas parts and service facilities located all over the world. Larry Flynn, senior vice president of aircraft services who was brought in by Boisture, said, "There's no question that service sells airplanes." Gulfstream's service side is critical in improving aircraft that are still on the assembly line, he explained. Rather than wait for information to filter back from a fixed base operation (FBO), which may or may not be completely accurate, Gulfstream can get better data more quickly from its own shops.

Superior service had always been a point of pride with Gulfstream. In the growing number of service centers, Flynn spoke with customers and Gulfstream service employees. Together they developed a set of service standards for the company to meet and try to exceed. "This is a key in the service business," he said. "The right employees really know what needs to be done, and we set up standards to run through the whole service cycle, from the quote to getting an invoice out on time." [46]

Rollout of the GV

Moss arrived seven months prior to the rollout of the GV, which took place on September 22, 1995. By then, Gulfstream had secured orders from all over the world for the aircraft. The airplane emerged into the hot, steamy Savannah day amid a cloud of fog created by dry ice. The workers who had toiled under the uncertainty of the program and the company followed the airplane out of the hangar. Overhead, all four Gulfstream models flew by in formation to salute their newest sister.

During Gulfstream's darkest hours, the program was threatened because two questions loomed over the board of directors: Was there a sufficient market for the GV, and did the airplane's specifications guarantee that Gulfstream would hold on to its title as the premier builder of the business jet? History would show the answer to be yes on both counts, but it took the courage of the company's highest executives and the dedication of the shop workers to prove it.

A good day at Gulfstream. The flags signify that another aircraft has been sold. *(Photo courtesy of Gulfstream Aerospace.)*

CHAPTER ELEVEN

THE PINNACLE OF SUCCESS

1996–2000

"Gulfstream doesn't know what it can't do."

— Pres Henne, during the Gulfstream V rollout ceremony[1]

O N NOVEMBER 30, 1995, THE FIRST Gulfstream V soared from the runway, right on schedule. Employees and executives turned out to watch. Fred Breidenbach, president and COO of Gulfstream at the time, recalled the feeling: "Years of effort, all culminating in this very smooth, quiet takeoff. We were all yelling."[2]

Test pilots Gary Freeman and John O'Meara flew the airplane for an hour and 18 minutes in a flawless demonstration. "The GV flew really great; the engines were fantastic," O'Meara said later. "It's the kind of challenge that every test pilot dreams of."[3]

But it had been a long and turbulent journey for Gulfstream to get to this happy occasion. At first, the problems had been technical in nature. Careful design work gradually overcame these. The real question was one echoed throughout the history of Gulfstream: Was there a market for such an aircraft? With Gulfstream in such dire financial straits, the company's survival hinged on finding the right answer, and the decision to go forward was one of the riskiest Forstmann and the board of directors had to make. Ultimately, it was also one that secured Gulfstream's future as the world's premier manufacturer of business jets.

In the tradition of all the Gulfstream models, the design concepts for the GV began with Charles Coppi when the GIV was certified in 1987. What that next product should be was a hotly debated topic among engineers and management. The debate ranged from an entry-level 2,000-mile jet to the supersonic aircraft favored by Allen Paulson.

When the market had gone into its devastating tailspin three years later, the question turned from what type of aircraft the GV should be to whether a new airplane was needed at all. There was a feeling among Gulfstream's board of directors that the GIV already outclassed every business jet flying.

Then, in 1992, Bombardier had announced the Global Express, a business jet that the company claimed would vault over the GIV in performance and range to become the world's first ultra-long-distance business tool. "That triggered us to go forward because we felt we had a pretty fine airplane in the GIV," noted Robert Anderson, a member of Gulfstream's board of directors.

"As I can recall, we were not wildly enthusiastic about bringing out a GV, at least not early on, but we absolutely could not permit ourselves, as the premier executive jet builder in the world, to allow anyone else to build a longer range or better version of an executive jet."[4]

Gerard Roche, another board member, agreed: "If we're the Yankees, we knew that eventually we were going to meet the Braves in the World Series,"

The logo for the GV. The logo conveys elegance and speed.

he said. "They kept the tempo up for us to keep moving with due dispatch."[5]

Bombardier's announcement was not a formal one. It was merely a foreshadowing of the Canadian company's intent, and a production decision would not be made until 1993. Meanwhile, Gulfstream had been wrestling with itself over the design and the mission requirements of an ultra-long-range jet. One thought was to simply add more fuel to the GIV, but engineers quickly abandoned this brute force solution because it compromised almost all other performance values, including field lengths and maximum speed.

In early 1991, engineers, after considering and rejecting 16 different concepts, had settled on a GV design with the ability to fly 5,600 nautical miles. This, incidentally, was roughly the range of the planned Global Express and was only 1,000 miles longer than the GIV-SP's range. The approach taken was to improve the aerodynamic and structural efficiency of the GIV.

This concept had been dropped as well. Because Gulfstream had decided to continue production of the GIV-SP along with the new business jet, the planned GV would not generate new sales, an unacceptable situation. "This led to a total reevaluation of the V program," noted Sandra Horbach. "We had to differentiate them with a big enough price point to be able to sell both."[6] Chris Davis explained that the strategy was to keep the GIV-SP and the GV $10 million apart in price, and the cost had to follow.

Fortunately for Gulfstream, this was possible because fate had, once again, intervened in the form of a phone call from Rolls-Royce. In 1991, Senior Vice President of Engineering Charles Coppi had received a call from David Evans, the head of marketing at BMW/Rolls-Royce, a joint jet engine venture formed by the companies a year earlier. Evans wanted to brief Coppi on a new engine that was being conceived by the engine maker. Called the BR700 series, the engine line was to succeed the Tay, incorporating new technologies to make the power plant lighter and more fuel efficient and

A rendering of the BR710 engine. The BR700 series is a family of engines based on a common core. In 1990, BMW and Rolls-Royce set up a joint venture to develop a new generation of engines. Rolls-Royce later bought BMW's interest in the venture. *(Photo courtesy of Gulfstream Aerospace.)*

to give it greater takeoff thrust. The engine adapted the core of the V2500 engine, which powered a narrow-body aircraft such as the Airbus A320, A321, A319 and McDonnell Douglas MD90, with a lighter nacelle, making the package lighter overall.

The BMW/Rolls-Royce executives were intent on finding a launch customer for the engine. This gave Gulfstream's engineers a golden opportunity to get in early on the engine's design and have it fit their specifications, Coppi explained:

"We were confident they had made their intentions known to Bombardier. We would never have another chance to tailor an engine to precisely the aircraft's needs. Furthermore, the engine's design was based on the most reliable and technically proven Rolls-Royce engines in service — the V2500 core and the Tay wide-chord fan technologies. That combination and heritage fit very well into Gulfstream's product design philosophy."[7]

That summer, Gulfstream and BMW/Rolls-Royce worked closely together, and the result was the BR710-48 engine. The BR710 was rated at 14,750 pounds of thrust at takeoff. At cruising speed, fuel efficiency at Mach .80 was improved 11 percent compared to the Tay. Furthermore, the complete engine package, which includes the engine, nacelle, thrust reverser and accessories, was lighter than the Tay, noted John Boutell, in charge of the BR700 program. The engine itself is electronically controlled. A computer automatically adjusts the engine by monitoring output, fuel flow, temperature and other factors affecting the aircraft's performance. The overall improved performance gave Gulfstream the opportunity to match up city pairs such as New York–Tokyo and Jiddah–Washington, D.C.

In September 1992, a mock-up of the GV was unveiled at the Farnborough Air Show in England. Bill Lowe and Charles Coppi made the presentations formally announcing the go-ahead for the GV. Gulfstream committed to its production, beating Bombardier to the punch in both the formal announcement and the engine selection, which Bombardier eventually chose for its ultra-long-range airplane. But Bombardier was now second in line as a customer for an engine designed specifically for the GV.

The BR710 was designed using Cray supercomputers. Besides a new core, the BR710 sports a new 48-inch-diameter fan and a new combustion system. The time between overhauls is an estimated 7,000 hours. *(Photo courtesy of Gulfstream Aerospace.)*

The Mission

Covering the air show, a reporter for *Aviation International News* wrote that "It may seem incongruous that, with scant signs of an end to the prevailing global economic recession and with many corporations either closing their flight departments or indefinitely canceling plans to add to their fleets, U.S. manufacturer Gulfstream Aerospace should pick this week's Farnborough Air Show to launch a new upscale business jet which will sell for almost $30 million."[9]

The signs were hardly scant. The nation's economy was beginning to show signs of growth, and globalization was becoming more than just a catchword of corporate jargon. The economies of nations along the Pacific Rim were emerging, bringing vast market and business opportunities, and capitalism triumphed in Eastern Europe. Furthermore, the fall of the Soviet Union expanded the role of the United States as a stabilizing political and economic force in the world.

International air travel for business purposes provided, at best, spotty connections between out-of-the-way city pairs and raised serious concerns for security. An ultra-long-distance executive jet addressed these concerns with the added benefit

THE ROLLS-ROYCE STORY

AS THEY WORKED CLOSELY TOGETHER on the details for the BR710 engine, Sir Ralph Robins, the chairman of Rolls-Royce, and Ted Forstmann gradually developed a friendship based on mutual respect and personal trust. In a way, their friendship resembles the close relationship that has developed between the Gulfstream Aerospace and Rolls-Royce organizations over more than 42 years of working together. Robins, interviewed in 2000, reflected on that relationship:

"Gulfstream and Rolls-Royce go rather well together. These top-end executive airplanes, I think you could hardly have two better names together. There are, of course, differences. They are driven by their being an airframe company and we being an engine company. Also, we're a large company working across a wide range of products, from tiny 250 horsepower helicopter engines up to 110,000-pound-thrust turbofans, ship propulsion and power generation, and they are a two-product company. But what we've always liked about Gulfstream was that they recognized where their market opportunity was and produced a top-quality product to exploit that opportunity, and that was exactly our thinking on everything we do."

In May 1998, with the 40th anniversary event of the GI's first flight approaching, Rolls-Royce and Gulfstream decided to commemorate their long legacy of excellence together. The actual date of the 40th anniversary was August 15, and the idea was to get all five models of the Gulfstream together at the same place and at the same time. However, the Farnborough Air Show, which was being held two weeks later, made that impracticable. The celebration was held in September instead.

During the celebration, William Boisture presented Rolls-Royce with a Gulfstream window with the number 40 etched into the glass. He also gave a framed picture of the number 1,000 — formed by scores of Gulfstreamers — taken to commemorate the company's 1,000th delivery. For its part, Rolls-Royce gave Gulfstream a polished fan blade with the number 40 etched into the metal.

One of the most famous fighters of World War II was the Spitfire (above), powered by the Rolls-Royce Merlin engine. The Merlin also powered the P-51 Mustang, also one of the most celebrated fighters of the war. *(Photo courtesy of* Air Force Magazine.*)*

Rolls-Royce has been involved in aviation almost as long as it had been building the cars for which it is famous. In 1904, Henry Royce built his first motor car. That year, he met Charles Rolls, a London car dealer. The men agreed on a partnership: Royce Limited would build cars to be sold exclusively by C.S. Rolls & Company. Two years later, the Rolls-Royce company was established with its headquarters in Derby, England. That year, Rolls-Royce Limited introduced its first automobile, the famous six-cylinder, 50-horsepower "Silver Ghost."

Following the outbreak of World War I, the British War Department asked Henry Royce to build the Renault V8 aircraft engine. In 1914 the 250-horsepower Eagle entered service in the Royal Air Force. Two other types, the Hawk and the Falcon, soon followed. The com-pany eventually supplied half the total horse-power used in the air war by the Allies. After the war, the Rolls-Royce engine became the basis of civil aviation in Europe. In 1919, a Vickers Vimy, powered by twin Eagle engines, made the first transatlantic crossing by an airplane and the first flight from England to Australia.

Before Royce died in 1933, he started design work on a 1,000-horsepower engine that incorporated advances used in the power plant that won the Schneider Trophy in 1931. The result was the Merlin, which was used in the Spitfire and the P-51 Mustang fighters, two of the most successful fighters in World War II.

In 1945, Rolls-Royce entered the business aviation market with the Dart turboprop engine, which powered the Vickers Viscount, the world's first turboprop airliner. It was the Dart that powered the first Gulfstream. The design was so durable that this type of engine was manufactured by Rolls-Royce until 1987.

In 1990, Rolls-Royce formed a joint venture with BMW called BMW/Rolls-Royce. Its first engine was the BR-710, which was delivered to the venture's first customer in September 1995. In 1999, Rolls-Royce bought out the interest in the joint venture, based in Germany.

of performing as a flying office, complete with the latest in communications technology.

The GV was billed as "a global transport for winning business in a global economy."[8] Indeed, industry leaders were told that the aircraft would cruise at 51,000 feet with speeds up to Mach .90 and a maximum range of 6,500 nautical miles, thus making the GV capable of flying higher, faster and further than any other business jet in history.[10] The GV was designed to be longer, with a larger flight deck and more baggage compartment. It would also include a complete computerized office with satellite communications, making communication possible anywhere in the world. In the final analysis, the GV would be 24 percent better than the GIV in overall performance efficiency.

Reengineering Relationships

As engineers worked and reworked designs, Ted Forstmann had put together the executive team that included Horbach, Davis, Breidenbach, Boisture and later Moss. A war room was set up where these executives gathered for daily stand-up meetings focused on keeping the GV on track. The war room had the schedule and milestones needed to get the GV in the air on schedule. The stand-up meeting was just that, a meeting where everyone reported on his or her progress standing up. This kept everyone focused on the facts, the schedule, their progress and what action they needed to take, and cut down on needless discussion.

As work continued on the GV, Breidenbach was able to negotiate revenue-sharing deals with Fokker Aviation for the empennage; Northrop-Grumman for the wings (initially contracted with Vought prior to its acquisition); Sundstrand for the electrical power; AlliedSignal for the auxiliary power unit, environmental control and pressurization systems; and later Honeywell for the new, enhanced avionics package.

Under the agreement, Gulfstream negotiated a fixed percentage that would apply to each aircraft's revenue to determine the price the supplier was paid for its part or component. The agreements saved $180 million on development — a whopping 23 percent of the cost.[11]

Gulfstream meanwhile sought a program manager to see the GV to completion. Charles Coppi had fulfilled his commitment to complete the conceptual development of the GV and transition it to production development. Having done that, Coppi stepped aside, acted in an advisory capacity and then retired in 1996.

A strong leader was needed to continue the project, and Board Director Thomas Bell knew of a perfect candidate: Pres Henne. Henne had been the program manager on the McDonnell Douglas MD90 airliner project, which he wrapped up in 1994.

Bell called Henne and said, "You're done with the MD90, what are you going to do now? We have this new airplane we've launched but it really needs a program manager to drive it all the way through the development certification."[12]

Here was another chance for Henne to help guide a new standard of aircraft. He leaped at the chance and joined Gulfstream in 1994. When he arrived, Henne was struck by two things: The engineering staff was smaller than what he was used to, with correspondingly fewer specialists in a particular field, but the motivation was much, much higher. "I coined a phrase for it which I stated

during the rollout ceremony," he said. "I said, 'Gulfstream doesn't know what it can't do.' If we need to do something, we just go and do it. It doesn't require seven signatures."[13]

Under Henne, the GV met both its rollout and first flight dates, even when Henne insisted that engineers find a way to reduce drag by 3 percent. Working with the engineers, they hit the target with engine pylon modifications, a redesigned canopy and other drag improvements. Balancing his need to remain in a managerial role and his desire to become involved was a struggle, Henne recalled. "There were times I had to literally bite my tongue and convince myself to stay out of it," he said. "Sometimes

Right: Gulfstream officers celebrate the first flight of the GV. Pictured from left to right are test pilots Gary Freeman and John O'Meara; Bryan Moss; Fred Breidenbach; Bill Boisture; Chris Davis; Pres Henne; and Bob Cooper.

Below: Gulfstream employees celebrate the GV's provisional certification in 1996. Final certification took place in 1997. *(Photo courtesy of Gulfstream Aerospace.)*

I couldn't because there were instances where, with my background and experience, I was the most experienced guy to address a particular issue."[14]

The GV incorporated the Gulfstream tradition of designing within comfortable margins. "We worked very hard to make sure that the airplane hit its performance requirements, and we beat every guarantee," Henne said.

Overall, the GV employed a new wing, new empennage, new engines, a longer fuselage and a number of new systems. The new wing is 1,136 square feet, compared to the GIV's 950-square-foot wing. The overall span increased from 77.8 feet to 93.5 feet, though the sweep remained the same at 31 degrees. The larger wing allowed engineers to increase the fuel load from 29,500 pounds to 41,300 pounds.

Completed, the GV can carry 14 passengers in a business arrangement and a maximum of 19 passengers in a higher arrangement, with accommodations for up to four crew members. Its FAA takeoff distance is 6,100, and it can land on a runway just under 2,770 feet long. Its range, carrying eight passengers and four crew members, is 6,500 nautical miles at Mach .80. The cabin is 6 feet 2 inches high.

The GV was designed to meet Extended-Range Twin Operations (ETOPS) requirements, which meant that no single failure of any system would cause the crew to divert the airplane from its des-

The GV took its first flight on November 28, 1995. Although the engines were first flown on the Gulfstream V, the BR700 family will benefit from additional experience gained from airline operations on the MD-95, later known as the Boeing 717. *(Photo courtesy of Gulfstream Aerospace.)*

tination. This capability exceeds the requirement for business aircraft; ETOPS allows extended operations of twin engine aircraft on long routes over water or remote areas. With proven reliability and redundancy, an aircraft can fly within 180 minutes to an alternate airport at any given time.

New standards have been set inside the airplane as well. The avionics employ an optional Head-Up-Display system to ease the workload of pilots. This option was overwhelmingly chosen by customers because of the added safety and comfort.

The aircraft earned final FAA certification in 1997 following a rigorous testing program. To achieve certification, the aircraft were used full-time in a comprehensive 15-month flight test program, amassing more than 1,900 flight hours. "The certification process was tough because the rules and standards were more stringent, and the FAA was under intense political pressure at the time to be stricter on details," recalled Henne. "The inspectors really scrutinized the aircraft and the accompanying documentation."[15]

After certification, the GV arrived at the 1997 Paris Air Show following a triumphant world tour that claimed nine records for nonstop distance, speed and cruise altitude among large-cabin business aircraft.

An even greater testament to the aircraft's excellence, besides the growing number of orders, followed. The GV won the prestigious Robert J. Collier Trophy. In announcing the 1997 Collier Trophy, Steven J. Brown, president of the National Aeronautic Association, said, "The Gulfstream V, with its proven world-class altitude and range capabilities, demonstrates the value of innovative development and partnership strategies in today's global business environment."[16]

Longtime Gulfstreamer Knoxie Crocker, who was hired by Grumman in 1965 and became the first woman foreman at Gulfstream, was one of several hundred Gulfstream employees chosen to attend the ceremonies. "It was such an honor," said Crocker. "That was my highlight of everything I've done since I've been here."[17]

Rocketing Revenues

As the GV reaped awards and distinction, the company that had built it was reaping profits and recognition on Wall Street. Four years after its disastrous public offering, Gulfstream Aerospace went public again in October 1996. This time the company presented a very different picture. The IPO was the third largest that year on the New York Stock Exchange, netting more than $1 billion. The optimism of investors was well founded. In 1996, the company had a $3.3 billion backlog of orders and the first three GVs were delivered for interior completion. Besides the three GVs, twenty-four GIV-SPs were green-delivered. The pace of production was speeding up, and the company continued to refine its manufacturing process, a difficult task because the GV was being built alongside the GIV-SP.

When the GIV-SP was introduced, it took approximately 67 days from the time a fuselage was put on a wing to the time the green aircraft

was certified by the FAA. The production time was cut to less than 30 days. The manufacturing and design teams also developed a tooling concept which allowed 60 percent of the major tools to be used on both aircraft — even though virtually none of the assemblies were the same.[18]

The improved efficiencies showed immediate results. Gulfstream achieved record profits. Though revenue increased slightly to a record $1.06 billion (as compared to $1.04 billion the prior year) net income increased by 62 percent, from almost $29 million in 1995 to $47 million in 1996. Better still, the company had a firm backlog of 94 aircraft as of the end of 1996, representing $3.1 billion in revenue.[19]

The picture kept getting brighter. In 1997, Gulfstream was gearing itself up to deliver 51 aircraft, an 89 percent increase over the prior year. In addition to record delivery and backlog, Gulfstream was on its way to capturing 70 percent of the service and parts business for its aircraft. By the end of 1997 — Gulfstream's 39th year — revenues almost doubled to $1.9 billion. With the costs of research and development for the GV covered, net income skyrocketed to $243 million.[20]

In addition, Gulfstream aggressively pursued the completions market. In 1990, the company completed about 70 percent of the Gulfstream aircraft. By the mid-1990s, Gulfstream had captured nearly all of the completions. In 1998, Gulfstream enhanced its strength in the completions and service area with the $250 million acquisition of K-C Aviation, the leading independent large cabin and completions center. This added three service centers, located in Wisconsin, Massachusetts and Texas, and enabled the company to grow its completions business and expand its aircraft services.

Larry Flynn, senior vice president in charge of Aircraft Services, said he and Boisture had changed the way Gulfstream looked at service. "The mentality here had been, 'Here's the price and here's the

Gulfstream's Service Center in Brunswick, Georgia. Worldwide expansion and revamping of the service market captured 70 percent of the Gulfstream service and parts business. *(Photo courtesy of Gulfstream Aerospace.)*

The entrance to the $16 million Gulfstream Service Center in Savannah. *(Photo courtesy of Gulfstream Aerospace.)*

service.' There wasn't a real focus or interest in getting market share," he explained.

"The only salesmen they had were in the office, not traveling. So we changed that whole approach, marketing-wise, and then internally, with the leadership of the people. We brought on some good leadership, got them some tools and Bill got us a hangar."[21]

The sales force didn't sell for one location only; they sold the Gulfstream service package that applies at any location.

A New Beginning

When Grumman launched the GI in 1958, the company's original intention was to produce the airplane and leave the completions and service to others. It took a few visionaries such as

Albert "Goldie" Glenn to convince the organization that the company had both the opportunity and the responsibility to work with customers after the sale.

By 1998, this insight had been raised to a fine art. Under Forstmann, Davis, Boisture and others, a slew of products and services was established: Gulfstream Lease; Gulfstream Worldwide Service; Gulfstream ServiceCare; Gulfstream Financial Services; Gulfstream Shares; Gulfstream Pre-Owned Aircraft; Gulfstream Management Services; and Gulfstream Charter Services. More businesses had access to Gulfstream jets through leasing, time-share and chartering. In addition, for the first time corporations with aircraft could look to Gulfstream to manage their fleets. In terms of products and services, Gulfstream Aerospace bore little resemblance to its earlier incarnations.

These new areas not only contributed to another record-breaking year — $2.4 billion in revenue in 1998 — but they promised to ensure a stream of cash even during industry downturns.

Gulfstream extended its presence overseas to promising emerging markets. Asia, in particular, showed potential in spite of the severe recession

that region suffered in 1998. A marketing office was set up in Hong Kong, and in 1998 the GV was presented at the Singapore Air Show. The popularity of Gulfstream aircraft in these markets is not surprising; its range, versatility and durability have always made it popular in international markets. With the GV, Gulfstream locked up the market, especially in Asia. "The characteristics of the Gulfstream V make it the perfect product to match the requirements of Asian customers," noted Joseph Walker, senior vice president of sales and marketing. "The GV has flown nonstop from Singapore to London, Tokyo, Hawaii, Sydney, Johannesburg. In one stop, it can fly to any city in the Americas."[22]

In 1998, a second stock offering was launched with even more spectacular results. Eighteen million shares, about half of Forstmann Little's ownership, were sold at $43 a share, almost double the price of the successful 1996 IPO, raising close to $900 million. During the year, Forstmann assumed the title of CEO to go along with his responsibilities, the first time he formally accepted the mantle. He created an office of the chief executive that included Chris Davis as executive vice president and chief financial and administrative officer and Bill Boisture, appointed president and COO after Fred Breidenbach retired from Gulfstream in 1997.

Under the Umbrella

Forstmann's formal role as CEO did not last long. Like parents who had successfully reared a wayward but promising child, Forstmann and the board had to decide when to let Gulfstream go for the good of the employees and the stockholders.[23]

The decision was not easy because Forstmann had fallen in love with Gulfstream. "I just hated the idea of selling Gulfstream," he said in an interview. "I would like to have Gulfstream until I ended.... I love the people. Without them, there's no way we could have been as successful as we were. They are fabulous at what they do."[24]

In 1997, Bill Boisture was named president and chief operating officer of Gulfstream. Shortly after this announcement, Gulfstream engineered a merger with General Dynamics and celebrated the rollout of its 400th GIV and 100th GV.

He wasn't alone in his enthusiasm. Many of the directors on the board discovered they thoroughly enjoyed touring the manufacturing facility. "I've been down there twice at the invitation of Bill Boisture," noted Colin Powell. "It really didn't take much to get me to go. I had a lot of fun with the employees, signing autographs, taking pictures, giving pep talks."[25]

Powell said the issue uppermost in the minds of board members was finding a good home for the company. He recalled the meeting when Forstmann announced his intentions to find a parent for the company.

"Teddy made the case that we had reached a point in the maturation of the company where he'd pretty much done all he could do, and we had done all we could. For the company to grow, it made sense to merge it with a larger organization. The board agreed."[26]

On September 8, 1999, members of Gulfstream's board of directors met at Manhattan's famous French restaurant, Daniel, for a farewell dinner. The mood was poignant and the atmosphere emotional. "This was a ride I'll never forget," said Roger Penske. "These weren't just meetings because I looked forward to seeing these people." Seated, from left to right: Bryan Moss, Lynn Forester, Bob Strauss, Ted Forstmann, Roger Penske, Sandra Horbach, Chris Davis. Standing, from left to right: Nick Forstmann, Bob Anderson, Mark McCormack, Colin Powell, Bill Boisture, Drew Lewis, Charlotte Beers, Gerard Roche, Henry Kissinger, Donald Rumsfeld. Not pictured are Thomas Bell, Michael Ovitz, Allen Paulson and George Shultz.

Sandra Horbach said Gulfstream was unique in the history of Forstmann Little. "When you pour your blood and sweat and tears at that intensity, it is very hard to separate your personal feelings about the company from what the right thing to do is."[27]

In April 1999, Gulfstream and General Dynamics began discussing a possible merger. Meanwhile, Forstmann gave each employee stock options. By the middle of May, the details were hammered out and the announcement was made that the defense giant would purchase Gulfstream in a one-for-one stock swap. From the $850 million leveraged buyout in 1990, Gulfstream's value had ballooned to $5.3 billion when the deal was signed.

The announcement came as a surprise because General Dynamics had sold off Cessna just seven years earlier, a move that Nicholas Chabraja, who became CEO and chairman in 1997, viewed as a mistake. The defense company had also divested its F-16 fighter operation, handing the cash back to shareholders. "It looked like a slow-death liquidation," wrote a reporter in *Forbes*. "Indeed, up until 1993, everybody, from the Pentagon to Wall Street, assumed that the company was going to disappear."[28]

Instead, General Dynamics was revitalized. It purchased Advanced Technology Systems, Bath Iron Works, Teledyne Vehicle Systems and Nassco Systems. After the Gulfstream purchase,

General Dynamics reorganized into four divisions — Marine Systems, Combat Systems, Information Systems and Technology, and Aerospace. General Dynamics' presence in the military market is expected to help Gulfstream in its role as a supplier of special-mission government aircraft.

Coincidentally, by February 2000, the fourth GV was delivered to the U.S. government. Designated the C-37A, two of the four are assigned to the Air Force's 89th Airlift Wing. One is in use by the U.S. Army and the fourth was purchased for the Department of Defense's regional Commander-in-Chief support mission. Two more were ordered to be used for counterterrorism and disaster response missions. The aircraft's incredible range permits teams to travel all over the world at a moment's notice.

On July 30, 1999, the sale of Gulfstream to General Dynamics was finalized. "This is the beginning of a new and exciting chapter for Gulfstream," wrote Boisture and Davis in a joint letter to employees.

"Each and every one of you should feel proud in this accomplishment. It was not that many years ago when we were in a very tough business situation. We had built planes we couldn't sell and our world-class workforce had shrunk to 3,800 people. Since then our team — now 7,800 strong — has developed a broad set of products and services, become the model of efficiency in production and set the world standard for quality.... After working with the leadership of General Dynamics for the past few months, we are confident that the future is bright for our employees and our customers."[29]

The Future

Bryan Moss noted that as the GV matures, Gulfstream will find ways to improve the aircraft to make it more capable and more cost efficient. By 2000, for instance, Gulfstream was on track to getting certification on a revolutionary advancement for the HUD system. Called the Enhanced Vision System (EVS), it permits a pilot to see runway lights and terrain otherwise obscured by inclement weather by using a finely tuned, dual-band infrared camera. The EVS image is displayed on the HUD.

"For EVS believers," noted *Aviation Week & Space Technology*, "the Gulfstream program represents the end of a long struggle. At different times, engineers at a major avionics company and a major HUD supplier, and the director of the Federal Aviation Administration's synthetic-vision demonstration, have said outright that ... EVS cannot work."[30] The EVS system proved its worth during the National Business Aviation Association's 1999 show in Atlanta, where it debuted. Bad weather had reduced visibility to 250 feet, but the EVS permitted the pilot to see the runway lights as far out as 500 feet.[31]

Shortly after the 1999 NBAA conference, the GV captured its 60th world record. A fully equipped GV, with three passengers and four crew members, flew from Beijing to Houston, setting the record for the longest nonstop flight from Asia to the United States. The GV flew a 6,471-nautical-mile route that was completed in 13 hours and 21 minutes. It cruised at Mach .8 at 51,000 feet and landed with NBAA IFR fuel reserves. "It was not flown with the objective of setting the 60th Gulfstream V world record," noted Joe Walker. "This flight was made in a fully outfitted aircraft in the course of a normal business day as a productive business tool for the executives on board."[32]

As the GIV-SP and the GV continue to soar, Gulfstream Aerospace is committed to finding ways to exceed the expectations of its customers. "There will be services we can still do to make the aircraft better and more cost effective," noted Bryan Moss.

One of the most exciting areas where Gulfstream is leading the market is in the practical use of the Internet. In September 1999, Gulfstream established an online spare parts/service support system. Operators can now order parts or service anywhere in the world, anytime during the day or night.

Less than four months later, Gulfstream made history with the first sale of a new aircraft over the Internet. Mark Cuban, cofounder of broadcast.com, purchased a GV for $40 million, which also made the transaction the single largest in the history of the Internet. Cuban toured Gulfstream's Website, moving from the pre-owned area to the GIV-SP and then the GV. A demonstration flight was coordinated electronically as well, although the actual demo took place in a real GV.[33]

Gulfstream
Gulfstream
100th GV
Gulfstream
400th GIV
Gulfstream
Gulfstream
Gulfstream

Opposite: The early 2000 joint rollout of the 400th GIV and the 100th GV was a major success. The company had been coproducing the two aircraft since 1995, while the aircraft continue to set records around the world. *(Photo courtesy of Gulfstream Aerospace.)*

Embracing and adapting the Internet — and any other new technology — to the needs of Gulfstream's customers is part of the entrepreneurial spirit that Boisture said he and Davis want to ensure is not lost at Gulfstream. "We don't want to forget that risk is what got us where we are and that the individual interest in the care of our customers is at the core of this business," he said.[34]

The future of Gulfstream Aerospace remains bright, but the next step in aircraft design is under study. Currently, Gulfstream and Lockheed Martin are looking at the technical, legal, environmental and marketing aspects of developing a supersonic business jet. The GV has so far obviated the need for an aircraft with greater ranges, but the speeds have remained subsonic. Once again, the familiar question is being asked: Is there a market for a business airplane that could potentially cost $60 million or more?

Whatever the future holds for Gulfstream, the company — its traditions begun by people like Goldie Glenn, Allen Paulson and Charles Coppi and reinvented by Ted Forstmann and his team — will continue to set the standards in the industry and inflame the passions of those associated with the company and the aircraft.

The technology has changed dramatically from the time Leroy Grumman envisioned building an aircraft for the pursuit of business, but the goal has never changed: To allow people in far-flung regions to develop the trust, through personal contact, that is necessary for business to succeed. No matter how the field of communications changes, nothing will replace the need for people to be able to sit face to face with one another and build personal relationships. And Gulfstream will continue to design and build business jets second to none.

At the rollout of the 100th Gulfstream V and 400th Gulfstream IV on April 25, 2000, Boisture said, "Today's celebration is a testimony to the excellence of our aircraft and the professionalism of the people who produce them. Over the 42-year history of our company, Gulfstream aircraft have earned the reputation as the world standard for safety, reliability, technical superiority, comfort and performance."

With its hard-earned and well-deserved reputation, Gulfstream now stands as one of the most widely known and respected brands in the world.

NOTES TO SOURCES

Chapter One

1. Charles Coppi, interview by the author, tape recording, 27 August 1999, Write Stuff Enterprises.
2. Robert A. Searles with Robert B. Parke, *NBAA's Tribute to Business Aviation* (National Business Aviation Association, 1997), 2.
3. Ibid.
4. Donald M. Pattillo, *A History in the Making: 80 Turbulent Years in the American General Aviation Industry* (McGraw-Hill, 1988), 2.
5. *Two Hundred Years of Flight in America: A Bicentennial Survey* (San Diego: American Astronautical Society, 1979), 156.
6. Searles and Parke, *NBAA's Tribute to Business Aviation*, 6.
7. Jeffrey L. Rodengen, *The Legend of Halliburton* (Fort Lauderdale, Florida: Write Stuff Enterprises, 1996), 30.
8. Roger Bilstein, *The American Aerospace Industry: From Workshop to Global Enterprise* (New York: Simon & Shuster Macmillan, 1996), 27.
9. Searles and Parke, *NBAA's Tribute to Business Aviation*, 26–27.
10. Roger E. Bilstein, *Flight in America 1900–1983* (Baltimore: John Hopkins University Press, 1984), 195.
11. Drew Fetherston, "Raising Grumman," *Newsday*, 19 April 1998, H15.
12. "Grumman 50 Years," Grumman marketing brochure.
13. Richard Thruelsen, *The Grumman Story* (New York: Praeger Publishers, 1976), 36.
14. "Grumman 50 Years," Grumman marketing brochure.
15. Lawrence M. Mead, Charles Coppi, and John Strakosch, "A Case Study by Grumman Aerospace Corporation and Gulfstream American Corporation on the Gulfstream III," June 1980, 3–4.
16. Ibid., 4.
17. Ibid.
18. René J. Francillon, *Grumman Aircraft Since 1929* (Putnam Aeronautical Books, 1989), 96.
19. Bill Gunston, *Grumman: Sixty Years of Excellence* (Orion Books, 1988), 24.
20. Ibid.
21. Thruelsen, *The Grumman Story*, 127.
22. Ibid., 138.
23. Ibid., 127.
24. Ibid.
25. Ibid.
26. "Leroy Grumman, the Builder of Aeronautics Giant Dies," *New York Times*, 5 October 1982, D25.
27. Donald S. Lopez in Association with the National Air and Space Museum, *Aviation, from Our Earliest Attempts at Flight to Tomorrow's Advanced Designs* (Macmillan, 1995), 124, 137.
28. "Grumman 50 Years," Grumman marketing brochure.
29. *Two Hundred Years of Flight*, 124.
30. S. Saunders & I.A. Woodhouse, *The Grumman Gulfstreams* (Berkshire, England: LAAS International, 1979), 3.
31. Francillon, *Grumman Aircraft Since 1929*, 267.
32. Mead, Coppi, and Strakosch, "A Case Study," 4.
33. Coppi, interview, 27 August 1999.
34. Ibid.
35. Ibid.
36. Charles Coppi, *Gulfstream's Heritage, Creating the Gulfstream I*, oral history, 2.

Chapter One Sidebar

1. Thruelsen, *The Grumman Story*, 323.
2. Bob Smyth, interview by Alex Lieber, tape recording, 19 November 1999, Write Stuff Enterprises.
3. "Leroy Randle Grumman," *Grumman Plane News*, special memorial issue, October 1982.
4. Ibid.

Chapter Two

1. Coppi, *Gulfstream's Heritage*, 2.
2. Ibid.
3. Ibid.
4. Coppi, interview, 27 August 1999.
5. Coppi, *Gulfstream's Heritage*, 2.

6. Ibid.
7. Peter Viemeister, interview by Lynda Natali, tape recording, 28 September 1999, Write Stuff Enterprises.
8. *Gulfstreamer,* fall 1978, 8–9.
9. Coppi, interview, 27 August 1999.
10. Mead, Coppi, and Strakosch, "A Case Study," 4.
11. George Vitteritti, interview by the author, tape recording, 27 August 1999, Write Stuff Enterprises.
12. Coppi, interview, 27 August 1999.
13. Mead, Coppi, and Strakosch, "A Case Study," 4.
14. Viemeister, interview.
15. Coppi, *Gulfstream's Heritage,* 6.
16. "Gulfstream near Completion; 1st Flight in Mid-August," *Grumman Plane News,* 18 July 1958, 1.
17. Fred J. Knight, *Gulfstream: A Tribute to the Ultimate Biz-Jet 1958–1991* (The Self Publishing Association, Ltd., 1992), 14.
18. "Grumman's Propjet Gulfstream," *Flight Magazine,* November 1957, 32.
19. *Gulfstreamer,* fall 1978, 8, 9.
20. Viemeister, interview.
21. Bob Smyth, interview by Alex Lieber, tape recording, 9 November 1999, Write Stuff Enterprises.
22. Ibid.
23. Ibid.
24. Viemeister, interview.
25. Ibid.
26. Albert "Goldie" Glenn, interview by the author, tape recording, 27 August 1999, Write Stuff Enterprises.

27. Herman Schonenberg, interview by Alex Lieber, tape recording, 19 August 1999, Write Stuff Enterprises.
28. Glenn, interview, 27 August 1999.
29. Ibid.
30. Schonenberg, interview.
30. Ibid.
31. Ibid.
32. Thruelsen, *The Grumman Story,* 278.
33. Johan S. Marais, 1998, Gulfstream Customer Focus Article.
34. Ibid.
35. Ibid.
36. Ibid.
37. Ibid.
38. Ibid.

Chapter Three

1. "October 2, 1966," *Gulfstreamer,* summer 1976, 8.
2. Coppi, interview, 27 August 1999.
3. Ibid.
4. Mead, Coppi, and Strakosch, "A Case Study," 9.
5. Coppi, interview, 27 August 1999.
6. Information obtained from Charles Coppi, April 2000.
7. Schonenberg, interview.
8. Mead, Coppi, and Strakosch, "A Case Study," 10.
9. Saunders and Woodhouse, *The Grumman Gulfstreams,* 25.
10. "1991: Jubilee Year for the Gulfstream II," *Gulfstreamer,* fall/winter 1991, 3–7.
11. Coppi, interview, 27 August 1999.
12. Mead, Coppi, and Strakosch, "A Case Study," 10.

13. Schonenberg, interview.
14. Ibid.
15. Ibid.
16. Coppi, interview, 27 August 1999.
17. Ibid.
18. Ibid.
19. Ibid.
20. Ibid.
21. Peter Bacque, "Why Do Plane Styles Vary? Form Follows Function, Designers Explain," *Richmond Times Dispatch,* 4 September 1997, E-1.
22. Francillon, *Grumman Aircraft Since 1929,* 496.
23. "Grumman Gulfstream II Design Summary," marketing brochure, February 1965.
24. Smyth, interview, 19 November 1999.
25. Ibid.
26. "October 2, 1966," 8.
27. Ibid.
28. Ibid.
29. Ibid.
30. Ibid.
31. Ibid.
32. Ibid.
33. Ibid.
34. Information provided by Bob Smyth, April 2000.
35. Ibid.
36. Ibid.
37. Francillon, *Grumman Aircraft Since 1929,* 496.
38. "Corporate Experience Aids Gulfstream 2," *Aviation Week & Space Technology,* 9 October 1967, 56.
39. Ibid.
40. "40th Anniversary," *Business & Commercial Aviation,* January 1998, 52.
41. Francillon, *Grumman Aircraft Since 1929,* 499.
42. Knight, *Gulfstream: A Tribute,* 99–100.

43. Albert "Goldie" Glenn, interview by Lynda Natali, tape recording, 9 September 1999, Write Stuff Enterprises.
44. Grumman News Release, 8 April 1967.
45. "Bond Sale for Grumman Facility Underway," Grumman News Release, 23 August 1966.
46. Glenn, interview, 27 August 1999.
47. Schonenberg, interview.
48. Knight, *Gulfstream: A Tribute,* 99–100.
49. Glenn, interview, 27 August 1999.
50. Glenn, interview, 9 September 1999.
51. Fred J. Knight, *The Story of the Grumman Gulfstreams* (West Sussex, England: Henfield Press, 1979), 109.
52. Saunders and Woodhouse, *The Grumman Gulfstreams,* 29.
53. Joseph Anckner, interview by Lynda Natali, tape recording, 30 September 1999, Write Stuff Enterprises.

Chapter Four

1. Glenn, interview, 27 August 1999.
2. James M. Naughton, "Nixon Orders 90-Day Wage-Price Freeze," *New York Times,* 16 August 1971, 1.
3. "Grumman to Cut back on Production, Employees," *Savannah Evening Press,* 7 February 1970.
4. Francillon, *Grumman Aircraft Since 1929,* 35.
5. Ibid.
6. Glenn, interview, 9 September 1999.

7. "Grumman, One D...d Thing after Another," *Forbes,* 5 February 1979, 39.
8. Ibid.
9. Francillon, *Grumman Aircraft Since 1929,* 35.
10. Thruelsen, *The Grumman Story,* 365.
11. Gunston, *Grumman: Sixty Years of Excellence,* 125.
12. "American Av to Be Bought by Grumman," *Aviation International News,* September 1972, 1.
13. "Grumman, One D...d Thing," 39.
14. Ibid.
15. Russ Meyer, interview by the author, tape recording, 24 November 1999, Write Stuff Enterprises.
16. Glenn, interview, 9 September 1999.
17. Glenn, interview, 27 August 1999.
18. Ibid.
19. "Grumman to Expand Savannah Operation," *Savannah Evening Press,* 28 May 1975, 1.
20. S. Saunders and I.A. Woodhouse, *The Grumman Gulfstreams,* 30.
21. Ibid.
22. Francillon, *Grumman Aircraft Since 1929,* 501.
23. "Grumman, One D...d Thing," 39.
24. Meyer, interview.
25. "Grumman, One D...d Thing," 39.
26. Francillon, *Grumman Aircraft Since 1929,* 504.
27. Ibid.
28. "Grumman American," *Plane & Pilot,* December 1975, 41.
29. Ibid.
30. "Discover the Difference," *Grumman American Trainer,* marketing material.

31. Susan Crandell, "T-Cat Grumman: American's Teaching Machine Puts Challenge into the Game of Flight Training," *Flying,* October 1978, 90.
32. Francillon, *Grumman Aircraft Since 1929,* 524.
33. Ibid.
34. Ibid., 525.
35. Grumman American Aviation Corporation 1976 Annual Report, 4.
36. Mead, Coppi, and Strakosch, "A Case Study," 13.
37. Ibid., 3.
38. William A. Shumann, "Economy Delaying Fuel-Efficient Aircraft," *Aviation Week & Space Technology,* 15 September 1975, 38.
39. "GIII O.K. Deferred As Orders Pour In," *Aviation International News,* 10 January 1977, 3.
40. Saunders and Woodhouse, *The Grumman Gulfstreams,* 29.
41. Ibid.
42. Ibid.
43. Mead, Coppi, and Strakosch, "A Case Study," 33.
44. Francillon, *Grumman Aircraft Since 1929,* 498.

Chapter Five

1. "AJI and Allen Who?" *Aviation International News,* 11 August 1978, 12.
2. Matthew L. Wald, "Information Bank Abstracts," *New York Times,* 19 February 1978, 45.
3. "Grumman: One D...d Thing," 39.
4. John F. Berry, "Aircraft Refitter's Financial Angel,"

Washington Post, 30 July 1978, G1.

5. Ibid.
6. "Grumman: One D...d Thing," 39.
7. "Business Jet Competition Intensifies," *Aviation Week & Space Technology*, 27 June 1977, 57.
8. "Grumman American Aviation President Speaks to Employees," *Southern Exposure*, 20 December 1977, 1.
9. "Record Sales Build Hefty Backlog into 1980," *Aviation Week & Space Technology*, 26 September 1977, 48.
10. Mead, Coppi, and Strakosch, "A Case Study," 4.
11. Allen Paulson, interview by the author, tape recording, 28 September 1999, Write Stuff Enterprises.
12. Meyer, interview.
13. "Grumman: One D...d Thing," 39.
14. Information provided by Bob Smyth, April 2000.
15. Glenn, interview, 27 August 1999.
16. "AJI and Allen Who?" 12.
17. Schonenberg, interview.
18. Peter Viemeister, *Start All Over: An American's Experience* (Bedford, Virginia: Hamilton's, 1995), 334–335.
19. Ibid.
20. Ibid., 344.
21. Paulson, interview.
23. Lee Honeycutt, "Allen Paulson: Aviation's Rags to Ritches Story," *Southern Horizons*, 16 January 1984.
24. "The Used-Airliner King," *Newsweek*, 13 January 1969, 73.
25. Ibid.

26. *Sky*, March 1984, 45–48.
27. John F. Berry, "Aircraft Refitter's Financial Angel," G1.
28. Ibid.
29. "Paulson Vows No Changes after Grumman Sale," *Aviation International News*, 12 September 1978, 74.
30. "Three Aircraft Added, One Cut by Gulfstream," *Aviation Week & Space Technology*, 11 December 1978, 72.
31. Ibid.

Chapter Six

1. Dan Murphy, interview by Lynda Natali, tape recording, 1 December 1999, Write Stuff Enterprises.
2. Kenneth Labich, "The Turkey That Learned to Soar," *Fortune*, 30 May 1983, 58.
3. Steven Rattner, "Anti-Inflation Plan by Federal Reserve Increases Key Rate," *New York Times*, 7 October 1979, 1.
4. PR Newswire, 23 September 1980.
5. Rush Loving Jr., "How the Airlines Will Cope with Deregulation," *Time*, 20 November 1978, 38.
6. Norman Wilson, interview by Alex Lieber, tape recording, 2 March 2000, Write Stuff Enterprises.
7. Bill Bauer, interview by Lynda Natali, tape recording, 1 December 1999, Write Stuff Enterprises.
8. "Outfitting Center Nears Completion," *Southern Exposure*, 25 April 1980, 1.

9. Ibid.
10. Labich, "The Turkey That Learned to Soar," 58.
11. "Gulfstream to Expand, Sell Piston Line," *Aviation Week & Space Technology*, 21 May 1979, 20, 21.
12. "Outfitting Center Nears Completion," 1.
13. "Gulfstream III Rollout Cuts Ribbons in Savannah," *Aviation International News*, 25 September 1979, 1.
14. Ibid.
15. Ibid.
16. Ibid.
17. "Gulfstream III Emerges; November First Flight," *Aviation International News*, 1 November 1979, 16.
18. Bob Smyth, interview by Alex Lieber, tape recording, 8 December 1999, Write Stuff Enterprises.
19. Mead, Coppi, and Strakosch, "A Case Study," 44.
20. PR Newswire, 28 April 1980.
21. Michael Hardy, *Sea, Sky and Stars: An Illustrated History of Grumman Aircraft* (Dorset, England: Arms and Armour Press, 1987), 125.
22. "Gulfstream to Expand," 20–21.
23. Ibid.
24. Bob Coman, interview by Lynda Natali, tape recording, 20 October 1999, Write Stuff Enterprises.
25. "Gulfstream to Expand," 20–21.
26. "Grumman American Stretching Gulfstream G-1," *Aviation Week & Space Technology*, 17 September 1979, 27.
27. Coman, interview.

28. "Intercom," *FAA Southern Region,* 13 November 1980, 1.
29. Ibid.
30. Ibid.
31. Coman, interview.
32. Knight, *Gulfstream: A Tribute,* 94.
33. Howard Banks, "They're Welcome to It," *Forbes,* 28 March 1983, 82.
34. Coman, interview.
35. "Tesoro Petroleum: The Irony of Becoming a Takeover Target," *Business Week,* 6 October 1980, 61.
36. Ibid.
37. Bob Cooper, interview by Lynda Natali, tape recording, 4 November 1999, Write Stuff Enterprises.
38. "Peregrine—Primary Air Force Trainer," *Southern Exposure,* 25 March 1982, 2.
39. "First Flight of Peregrine Trainer Scheduled," *Aviation Week & Space Technology,* 4 May 1981, 56.
40. "Gulfstream Completes Rockwell Unit Purchase," *Aviation Week & Space Technology,* 9 February 1981, 32.
41. "GAD Sale to Gulfstream Completed Feb. 3," *Aviation International News,* 1 March 1981, 1.
42. Cooper, interview.
43. Gulfstream chronology, provided by Gulfstream Aerospace.
44. "Gulfstream Grows; Aims for Fortune 500 Listing," *Savannah News-Press,* 23 May 1982, E1.
45. "Gulfstream III Sets Around-World Record," *Southern Exposure,* 25 March 1982, 3.

46 "President's Message," *Southern Exposure,* 23 November 1982, 1.

Chapter Seven

1. "Corporate Aviation, '85: Besieged but Unbowed," *Dun's Business Month,* August 1985, 61.
2. "100th Gulfstream III Rolls off the Line," *Southern Exposure,* 2 September 1983, 3.
3. "40th Anniversary," 52.
4. "Rolls Engines Still Can't Generate Profits," *Business Week,* 21 March 1983, 45.
5. Albert "Goldie" Glenn, interview by Alex Lieber, tape recording, 7 December 1999, Write Stuff Enterprises.
6. "Chrysler May Want to Sell Gulfstream, but Paulson Has No Plans to Call It a Day," *Wall Street Journal,* 8 December 1989.
7. "By Landing Gulfstream on Wall Street, the Company's Chief Cashes In," *New York Times,* 1 May 1983.
8. "Gulfstream Workers Get Nearly $1,000 in Stock," *Savannah Morning News,* 21 April 1983, D1.
9. Ibid.
10. Glenn, interview, 7 December 1999.
11. "Just Like the Good Old Days," *Forbes,* 25 April 1983, 43.
12. "100th Gulfstream III Rolls," 3.
13. Hardy, *Sea, Sky and Stars,* 126.
14. Coman, interview.
15. Charles Coppi, interview by Alex Lieber, tape recording, 27 December 1999, Write Stuff Enterprises.

16. Coman, interview.
17. "GAC Receives U.S. Air Force C-SAM Contract," *Southern Exposure,* 1 July 1983, 2.
18. Ibid.
19. Ibid.
20. "C-20A Delivery and Acceptance Ceremony," *Southern Exposure,* 28 October 1983, 3.
21. Ibid.
22. Gulfstream Aerospace Corporation, Third Quarter Report, Management Discussion and Analysis.
23. Gene G. Marcial, "Gulfstream May Be Ready to Soar Again," *Business Week,* 10 September 1984, 120.
24. "Paulson Gambles on Steel, Horses," *Professional Pilot,* September 1983, 32.
25. "Son of Gulfstream Corp. President Foils Kidnapping," United Press International, 12 December 1983.
26. Pattillo, *A History in the Making,* 161.
27. "Corporate Aviation, '85: Besieged but Unbowed," 61.
28. Ibid.
29. Marcial, "Gulfstream May Be Ready," 120.
30. "Corporate Aviation, '85: Besieged but Unbowed," 61.
31. "Department of the Month: Field Service," *Southern Exposure,* March 1984, 8.

Chapter Eight

1. "Gee-IV, Step Down G-III. The Throne Belongs to the Gulfstream IV," *Flying,* January 1987, 62.
2. Charles Coppi, interview by Lynda Natali, tape

recording, 10 November 1999, Write Stuff Enterprises.

3. Ibid.
4. "Hushing the GII Spey," *Aviation International News,* 6 September 1974, 1.
5. Sir Ralph Robins, interview by Alex Lieber, tape recording, 3 March 2000, Write Stuff Enterprises.
6. Coppi, interview, 10 November 1999.
7. "Hushing the GII Spey," 1.
8. Coppi, interview, 10 November 1999.
9. "Rolls Keys Tay Engine Schedule to Fokke, 100/Gulfstream 4 Needs," *Aviation Week & Space Technology,* 4 March 1985, 27.
10. Coppi, interview, 10 November 1999.
11. Stanley W. Kandebo, "Rolls' Tay Engine Meets Schedule for Gulfstream 4 First Flight," *Aviation Week & Space Technology,* 23 September 1985, 103.
12. Coppi, interview.
13. Paul Proctor, "Gulfstream 4 Certification Expected This September," *Aviation Week & Space Technology,* 3 March 1986, 42.
14. Ibid.
15. "GIV Gulfstream Goes Further," *Flight International,* 14 September 1985, 30.
16. "Gee-IV, Step Down G-III," 62.
17. Scott Ticer, "Why Gulfstream's Rivals Are Gazing up in Envy," *Business Week,* 16 February 1987, 66.
18. Ted Mendenhall, interview by Alex Lieber, tape recording, 4 January 2000, Write Stuff Enterprises.

19. Ibid.
20. Ed Flynn, interview by the author, tape recording, 27 August 1999, Write Stuff Enterprises.
21. Knight, *Gulfstream: A Tribute,* 198.
22. "Gulfstream IV Rolls Out," *Gulfstream Savannah News,* 11 September 1985, 1.
23. Charles Coppi, interview by Alex Lieber, tape recording, 7 January 2000, Write Stuff Enterprises.
24. Bob Smyth, interview by Alex Lieber, tape recording, 12 December 1999, Write Stuff Enterprises.
25. "Gulfstream IV Here 2 Days after Maiden Flight," *Aviation International News,* 24 September 1985, 1.
26. "Gee-IV, Step Down G-III," 62

Chapter Nine

1. James Braham, "Iacocca Lifts Bizjets: But Don't Call Gulfstream the Cadillac," *Industry Week,* 14 October 1985, 21.
2. Ibid.
3. Ibid.
4. Paulson, interview.
5. "Paulson's Decision to Sell May Stem from Steel Firm," *Wall Street Journal,* 3 June 1985, A4.
6. Glenn, interview, 7 December 1999.
7. Bob Smyth, interview by Alex Lieber, tape recording, 22 December 1999, Write Stuff Enterprises.
8. Bauer, interview.
9. *Savannah Morning News,* 5 September 1986, C2.
10. Ibid., C1.
11. Knoxie Crocker, interview by David Patten, tape

recording, 30 November 1999, Write Stuff Enterprises.
12. Ibid.
13. Ibid.
14. "G'stream Service Center Fully Ensconced at LGB," *Aviation International News,* 2 October 1986.
15. "Gulfstream to Unveil Good News for Chrysler Shareholders," *Savannah Morning News,* 21 May 1987, A1.
16. Glenn, interview, 7 December 1999.
17. "Paulson Flies the GIV In," *Flight International,* 12 October 1985, 25.
18. "Gulfstream Circles World the Hard Way: 45 Hr, 26 Min," *Aviation International News,* 16 June 1987, 1.
19. "Gulfstream Jet Does It Again!" *Savannah News-Press,* 28 February 1988, C1.
20. "How Paulson's Pursuit Nosed out Lacy's SP," *Aviation International News,* 1 May 1988.
21. Ibid.
22. "Paulson Wins Horatio Alger Award," *Savannah Morning News,* 11 March 1985, B1.
23. "Wright Brothers Memorial Trophy Awarded to Gulfstream's Chairman/CEO," *Gulfstream Special,* December 1987, 1.
24. James Risen, "Gulfstream Is Acquired by Chrysler," *Los Angeles Times,* 20 June 1985, 1.
25. "Gulfstream Is Fitting SATCOMS on Business Jets for Corporate Customers," *Mobile Satellite Reports,* 17 October 1988, 1.

26. "Mach-2 Business Jet," *Popular Mechanics*, January 1989, 16.
27. Ibid.
28. Wendy Zellner and Chuck Hawkins, "Chrysler Heads Back to Earth," *Business Week*, 18 December 1989, 46.
29. Glenn, interview, 7 December 1999.
30. Daniel Kadlec, *Masters of the Universe* (HarperCollins, 1998), 170.
31. Andrea Rothman, "Ted Forstmann Doesn't Have to Say 'I Told You So,'" *Business Week*, 5 March 1990, 77.
32. Kadlec, *Masters of the Universe*, 174.
33. Paulson, interview.
34. Kadlec, *Masters of the Universe*, 175.

Chapter Ten

1. Sandra Horbach, interview by the author, tape recording, 15 October 1999, Write Stuff Enterprises.
2. Rita Koselka, "Let's Make a Deal," *Forbes*, 27 April 1992, 62.
3. Eric Weiner, "Corporate Jets: The Ultimate Status Symbol Still Sells," *New York Times*, 30 September 1990, section 3, p. 4.
4. "Despite Debt, Reduced Backlog, Paulson Optimistic about Gulfstream's Outlook," *Weekly of Business Aviation*, 26 March 1990, 97, 98.
5. "Gulfstream to Cut Workforce," *Savannah Morning News*, 24 April 1990, 1.

6. Ibid.
7. "Gulfstream Continues Its Belt-tightening," *Savannah Morning News*, 29 April 1990, 1.
8. "Duty in the Gulf War," *Gulfstreamer*, spring–summer 1991, 3.
9. Wade J. Kearns, Major, USAF, in a letter to the *Gulfstreamer*, fall–winter 1991, 15.
10. "Duty in the Gulf War," 6.
11. Ibid.
12. Anthony Bianca and William Symonds, "Gulfstream's Pilot," *Business Week*, 14 April 1997, 64.
13. Kay Williams Graves, "Gulfstream's New Flight Plan," *Georgia Trend*, February 1993, 40.
14. Paulson, interview.
15. Horbach, interview.
16. Kadlec, *Masters of the Universe*, 179.
17. Horbach, interview.
18. Graves, "Gulfstream's New Flight Plan," 40.
19. Kadlec, *Masters of the Universe*, 179.
20. Chris Davis, interview by the author, tape recording, 30 November 1999, Write Stuff Enterprises.
21. Horbach, interview.
22. Davis, interview.
23. Horbach, interview.
24. Fred Breidenbach, interview by the author, tape recording, 1 January 2000, Write Stuff Enterprises.
25. Ted Forstmann, interview by the author, tape recording, 15 October 1999, Write Stuff Enterprises.
26. Davis, interview.
27. Breidenbach, interview.

28. Ibid.
29. Ibid.
30. Bill Boisture, interview by the author, tape recording, 30 November 1999, Write Stuff Enterprises.
31. Ibid.
32. Ibid.
33. Andrea Rothman, "Ted Forstmann Doesn't Have to," 77.
34. Daniel Stoffman, "Bombardier's Billion-Dollar Space Race," *Canadian Business*, June 1994, 91.
35. Boisture, interview.
36. Tom Bell, interview by the author, tape recording, 2 February 2000, Write Stuff Enterprises.
37. Michael Ovitz, interview by the author, tape recording, 9 January 2000, Write Stuff Enterprises.
38. Ibid.
39. Davis, interview.
40. Ken Burkhart, interview by the author, tape recording, 11 November 1999, Write Stuff Enterprises.
41. "Record Order Placed for Gulfstream 4-SP," *Aviation Week & Space Technology*, 23 January 1995, 64.
42. Boisture, interview.
43. Marsha Grovenstein, interview by David Patten, tape recording, 30 November 1999, Write Stuff Enterprises.
44. Bryan Moss, interview by the author, tape recording, 29 November 1999, Write Stuff Enterprises.
45. Ibid.
46. Larry Flynn, interview by the author, tape recording, 30 November 1999, Write Stuff Enterprises.

Chapter Ten Sidebar

1. "Goldie Has the Right Stuff," *Savannah News-Press*, 27 November, 1983, 4E.
2. Ibid.
3. Ibid.
4. Ibid.
5. Goldie Glenn Scholarship.

Chapter Eleven

1. "Global Jet for Global Economy," *Aviation International News*, 10 September 1992, 3.
2. Breidenbach, interview.
3. "Flying High," *Leading Edge*, December 1995, 3.
4. Robert Anderson, interview by the author, tape recording, 22 December 1999, Write Stuff Enterprises.
5. Gerard Roche, interview by the author, tape recording, 14 October 1999, Write Stuff Enterprises.
6. Horbach, interview.
7. Charles Coppi, "The Gulfstream V: Pinnacle of the Legacy," January 2000, 3.
8. "Global Jet for Global Economy," 3.
9. Ibid.
10. "A Peek into the Future," *Leading Edge*, October 1992, 1.
11. "Gulfstream's Pilot," *Business Week*, 14 April 1997, 64.
12. Pres Henne, interview by David Patten, tape recording, 30 November 1999, Write Stuff Enterprises.
13. Ibid.
14. Ibid.
15. "Gulfstream V Earns Final FAA Certification," Gulfstream Update, Second Quarter '97, 1.
16. *Northrop Grumman News*, 27 February 1998.
17. Crocker, interview.
18. "Co-Production of the Gulfstream IV-SP and Gulfstream V," Gulfstream Update, Fourth Quarter '96, 4.
19. Gulfstream 1996 Annual Report, 2.
20. Gulfstream 1997 Annual Report, 2.
21. Flynn, interview.
22. Gulfstream press release, 22 February 2000.
23. Forstmann, interview.
24. Ibid.
25. Colin Powell, interview by the author, tape recording, 8 September 1999, Write Stuff Enterprises.
26. Ibid.
27. Horbach, interview.
28. Howard Banks, "Like a Phoenix," *Forbes*, 10 January 2000, 86.
29. "We've Joined General Dynamics," *Leading Edge*, 30 July 1999, 1.
30. Bill Sweetman, *Aviation Week & Space Technology*, 12 October 1999, 56.
31. Ibid., 12.
32. "GV Completes Longest Business Jet Flight from Asia to U.S.," *Business Wire*, 11 October 1999.
33. "Mark Cuban, Internet Pioneer, Buys New Gulfstream V Over the Web," *Business Wire*, 20 December 1999.
34. Boisture, interview.

INDEX

W.W. Boisture, Jr.
President and
Chief Operating Officer

Gulfstream Aerospace originated with a unique idea: to develop the first aircraft designed specifically for corporate business travel. That singular focus, to set the world standard for business aviation, is as true of our core business today as it was with the introduction of the Gulfstream I in the late fifties.

By maintaining a focus on excellence for over forty years, we have meticulously built a legacy of safety, reliability, technical superiority, comfort and performance. As a result, the Gulfstream brand stands among the very best in the world.

With today's Gulfstream IV-SP and Gulfstream V, we have developed aircraft with unprecedented performance. Since Gulfstream's inception, our goal has been to anticipate our customers' changing needs and consistently exceed their expectations — a goal pursued and met with great pride by the people of Gulfstream.

Enjoy reading <u>The Legend of Gulfstream</u>. If our history is any indication of our future, Gulfstream will remain the industry leader, an innovator, and a company focused on its customers' success for years to come.

Best regards,

VIII - MOM + DAD
PAGE 28 DAD (PHOTO)
PAGE 85 STORY (SOARING OVER OBSTACLES) DAD
PAGE 153 PHOTO "q" STAMP PHOTO